1953

THE NEWS
THE EVENTS
AND
THE LIVES
OF 1953

Elizabeth Absalom & Malcolm Watson

D'AZUR PUBLISHING

Published by D'Azur Publishing 2022
D'Azur Publishing is a Division of D'Azur Limited

The language, phrases and terminology within this book are as written at the time of the news reports during the year covered and convey the sentiments at that time. The news reports are taken from internationally recognised major newspapers and other sources of the year in question.
The language does not represent any personal view of the author or publisher.

First published in Great Britain in 2022 by D'Azur Limited
Contact: info@d-azur.com Visit www.d-azur.com
ISBN 9798357455185

ACKNOWLEDGEMENTS
The publisher wishes to acknowledge the following people and sources:

British Newspaper Archive; The Times Archive; Cover Malcolm Watson; p9 Malcolm Watson; p10 Quatro Valvole; p13 NASA; p18 Kaffe-netz; p22 G Plan; p24 Michelle McEwen on Unsplash; p29 Jan Canty on Unsplash; p31 Terry Goss; p37 seaforces.org; p39 From A Painting By George Hayter; p47 Genuine Army Surplus; p47 LinnkedIN; p51 Sovereign Rarities; http://maundymoney.info; p53 guildford-cathedral.org: P55 By Hannes Grobe 19:27, 20 June 2007 (UTC), Alfred Wegener Institute for Polar and Marine Research, Bremerhaven, Germany,; p57 coincraft.com; p57 Royal Mint; p61 RCMP Historical Collection; p65 Amusing planet; p73 British-sweets-blog; p75 Holiday Nepal Trek; p75 TseRigs (traditional Dress); p83 Young Sound, DanNav - Own work: p87 Tesco; p91 Barts Heritage; p91 open Sandwich; p91 Calendar Customs; p93 Live Blackpool; p95 Mumbaipsytrance; p97 Malcolm Watson; Whitstable Oyster Company; p99 Grant Crabtree - Grant Crabtree Photographic Collection; p99 https://www.familysearch.org; p105 Colnet; p105 Grimsby Live; p109 englandfootballonline.com; p111 spectaclemakers.com; p119 bottleoven. blogspot.com; p121 Popular Science Monthly Volume 82; Mike Peel (www.mikepeel.net);

Whilst we have made every effort to contact copyright holders, should we have made any omission, please contact us so that we can make the appropriate acknowledgement.

CONTENTS

LIFE IN 1953

Monarch: Queen Elizabeth II   Prime Minister: Sir Winston Churchill – Conservative (Knighted on 24 April)

In 1953, Winston Churchill was presiding over a period of rapid growth and increasing prosperity after the sombre years of the war. Towns and cities were reshaped by a massive building programme of council estates, tower blocks and shopping centres.

Rationing was still in place for some meats but most of the wartime restrictions had been lifted and life was becoming more comfortable. For the first time since the war petrol was off ration and a huge influx of cars took to the roads. Television sets mushroomed, taking up their now familiar place as the focal point of the 'sitting room' and the strange looking H-shaped aerials were clamped firmly to the chimney-stacks.

It was the year of the devastating North Sea Floods; the era of nuclear armament, Britain's atom bomb and the Cold War. Queen Elizabeth II was crowned; Mount Everest was conquered; the Korean War ended but British soldiers saw action in Egypt, Malaya and Kenya.

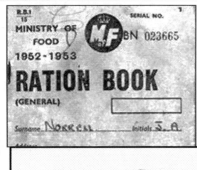

Hundreds died in the North Sea Floods

FAMOUS PEOPLE WHO WERE BORN IN 1953

20th April: Sebastian Foulkes, Novelist
6th May: Tony Blair, Politician
6th May: Graeme Souness, Scottish footballer
19th May: Victoria Wood, Performer
26th May: Michael Portillo, Politician
8th Aug: Nigel Mansell, Racing Driver
12th Oct: Les Dennis, Actor & Presenter
21st Oct: Peter Mandelson, Politician
16th Nov: Gryff Rhys Jones, Actor & writer

FAMOUS PEOPLE WHO DIED IN 1953

2nd Jan: Guccio Gucci, Founder of Fashion House
5th Mar: Joseph Stalin, Soviet leader
5th Mar: Sergei Prokofiev, Russian composer
24th March: Queen Mary, Consort of King George V
16th July: Hilaire Belloc, French born writer
28th Sep: Edwin Hubble, American astronomer
8th Oct: Kathleen Ferrier, British Contralto
9th Nov: Dylan Thomas, Welsh poet
27th Nov: Eugene O'Neill, Nobel Prize Laureate

HIGHLIGHTS OF THE YEAR

JANUARY
Dwight D Eisenhower is sworn in as the 34th President of the United States.
Devastating North Sea Floods on the east coast of Britain and the Netherlands.

FEBRUARY
James Watson and Francis Crick of the University of Cambridge announce their discovery of the structure of DNA.

MARCH
Queen Mary, consort of the late King George V dies in her sleep at Marlborough House.

APRIL
Prime Minister Winston Churchill is knighted by the Queen.
The Queen launches the Royal Yacht Britannia at John Brown Shipbuilders on the Clyde.

MAY
On the British Mount Everest Expedition, Edmund Hillary from New Zealand and Tenzing Norgay from Nepal become the first men to reach the summit of Mount Everest.

JUNE
The Coronation of Queen Elizabeth II takes place at Westminster Abbey.

JULY
The Korean War ends. The UN, China and North Korea sign an armistice agreement at Panmunjom. The north remains communist whilst the south remains capitalist.

AUGUST
The Ionian earthquake with a magnitude of 7.2 devastates Cephalonia and other islands.

SEPTEMBER
Sugar rationing ends in Britain.
US Senator John Fitzgerald Kennedy marries Jacqueline Lee Bouvier .

OCTOBER
The government sends troops to the colony of British Guiana blaming Communists for causing unrest. The constitution is suspended and a state of emergency declared.

NOVEMBER
In football, England loses 6–3 to Hungary at Wembley Stadium. Their first ever loss to a continental team at home.

DECEMBER
Sir Winston Churchill wins the Nobel Prize in Literature 'for his mastery of historical and biographical description and for brilliant oratory in defending exalted human values'.

FILMS AND ARTS

The 25th Academy Awards were held. Best picture is won by **The Greatest Show on Earth** set in the Ringling Bros. and Barnum and Bailey Circus. A circus troupe of 1,400 people appear, plus hundreds of animals and 60 railroad cars of equipment and tents.

From Here to Eternity, starring Burt Lancaster, Montgomery Clift and Frank Sinatra was released, dramatising Army life on a Hawaiian military base just prior to the Pearl Harbour attack.

British films included, **The Cruel Sea** with Jack Hawkins and **Genevieve** on the London to Brighton veteran car run.

The Crucible the drama by Arthur Miller, written as an allegory of McCarthyism, opened on Broadway.

The current affairs series **Panorama** is first shown on BBC. Sales of TV sets rise sharply in the weeks leading up to the **Coronation** in June. This was one of the earliest broadcasts to be deliberately recorded for posterity.

The publication of Ian Fleming's novel **Casino Royale** introduces James Bond to the world.

'The Moka', the Italian espresso coffee bar is the first to open in London and **Laura Ashley** sells her first printed fabrics.

1953 THE YEAR

In 1953, the standard rate of income tax was 47.5%; sweet rationing ended; the first James Bond novel, 'Casino Royale' was published by Ian Fleming; women applied 'Pancake Make-up' with a damp sponge and scarlet lipstick was the norm; duvets hadn't been heard of and beds had sheets and layers of blankets, all topped off with a nice thick eiderdown. Bedrooms were very cold ... on frosty nights, ice formed on the inside of the windows!; pubs closed at 10pm, and everybody seemed to smoke!

School boys wore short trousers and knee length socks, held up by elastic garters, and peaked school caps. Girls wore gym slips, shirts and ties and hats, and both wore blazers with the school badge.

Bombing during the war and the continuing demolition of urban slums meant more houses than ever were needed in a very short time. Council houses were the answer and in 1953 the country was undergoing a huge building programme set up by the government with a target of 300,000 new homes to be built each year. Central heating in houses was very rare and it was coal fires downstairs and electric fires or paraffin lamps, upstairs.

HOW MUCH DID IT COST?

The Average Pay:	£9 5s (£9.25) a week
The Average House:	£1,891
Loaf of White Bread:	7½d (3p)
Pint of Milk:	7d (3p)
Pint of Beer:	1s 11d (10p)
Dozen Eggs:	3s – 5s (15-25p)
Gallon of Petrol:	4s 6½d (23p)
Newspapers:	1½d–4d (up to 1½p)
To post a letter in UK:	2½d (1p)
B&W TV Licence:	£4 pa incl radio

Born in 1953, you were one of 50.75 million people living in Britain and your life expectancy *then* was 69.4 years. You were one of the 15.1 births per 1,000 population and you had a 2.8% chance of dying as an infant, most likely from an infectious disease such as polio, diphtheria, tetanus, whooping cough, measles, mumps or rubella. You were at the beginning of the country's recovery from the war, the decade that would transform Britain's social and cultural landscape. After the austerity, began an age of consumerism and when advertising was introduced on ITV, the nation could see the new products from the comfort of their own home. As prime minister Harold Macmillan famously said towards the end of the decade, "Most of our people have never had it so good."

YOU WERE BORN

POPULAR MUSIC

Frankie Lane was the singer of the year, **I Believe** topped the charts for 18 non-consecutive weeks and he had 8 top 10 entries, with 2 reaching No 1.

Both David Whitfield and Frankie Lane reached a joint top spot, with the same song, at the same time **Answer Me.**

FEBRUARY Guy Mitchell scored six top 10 singles, including the No1 **She Wears Red Feathers.**

MARCH The novelty song **How Much is That Doggie in the Window** gave Lita Roza a No1. Patti Page had a hit with it last year and it reached the Top Ten again for her in April.

JUNE **Terry's Theme**, an instrumental with music written by Charlie Chaplin for his film 'Limelight', made it to No 2 in the charts.

AUGUST Lyrics were put to **Terry's Theme** and as **Eternally**, Jimmy Young took it to No 8. In the US it was a hit for Vic Damone.

OCTOBER David Whitfield has his No1 with **Answer Me** followed by the same song by Frankie Lane two weeks later.

DECEMBER **I Saw Mommy Kissing Santa Claus** had a spell in the Top Ten over Christmas for the Beverley Sisters – at the same time as it was in the Top Ten for Jimmy Boyd.

A WORLD'S FIRST
THE CORONATION LIVE!

TOYS OF THE AGE

"Matchbox" toys were introduced by Lesney Products who gave the brand its name because the toys were sold in boxes similar to those in which matches were sold.

These were 'pocket money' toys and many boys (including the co-author!) soon built up large collections

The brand grew to encompass a broad range of toys, including larger scale die-cast models, plastic model kits and action figures.

1958 THE YEAR

In 1958 there were no state pre-schools or nurseries, so for most children at five years old, the first day at school was the first time they would have spent the day away from family or friends and for most, because their mother would have been home with them all day, the first time they would be separated. But for the child, school life had a routine – calling the register, lessons, playtime and mid-morning, the mostly dreaded, 'school milk'. Warmed by the sun or worse, when frozen, warmed by the radiator!

Reading, writing and arithmetic were most important; times tables were learnt by rote as was poetry; neat handwriting was practiced daily, and nature study was 'science' when leaves and acorns were identified and then later become 'arts and crafts'.

CHILDREN AT FIVE

In 1958 sweets came off ration and children with a few pennies pocket money could choose sweeties from the rows of jars on the shelves. Four blackjacks or fruit salads for a penny, a Barratt's Sherbet Fountain with a stick of liquorice in it, raspberry drops, dolly mixture or toffees.

You could 'smoke' a sweet cigarette whilst reading Dan Dare's adventures in Eagle or laugh with Radio Fun, Beano and Dandy comics.

HOW MUCH DID IT COST?

The Average Pay:	£483	(£9.30 p.w)
The Average House:	£2,058	
Loaf of White Bread:	11d	(5p)
Pint of Milk:	8d	(3p)
Pint of Beer:	2s	(10p)
12 months Road Tax	£12 10s	(12.50)
Gallon of Petrol:	5s 8d	(28p)
Newspapers:	3d - 6d	(1p- 2p)
To post a letter in UK:	3d	(1p)
TV Licence	£4 black & white	

YOU WERE FIVE

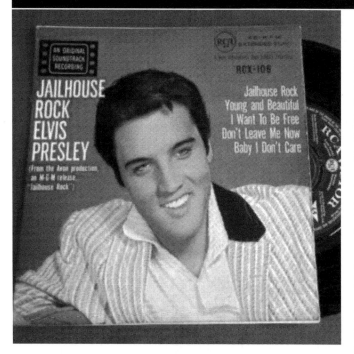

JUNE The Everly Brothers had three top 10 entries including **All I Have to Do is Dream** which spent seven weeks at No 1.

JULY Marty Wilde had his first chart hit with **Endless Sleep** a teenage 'tragedy' song, a hit in the US by Jody Reynolds, but originally thought by record companies as 'too depressing'.

OCTOBER Cliff Richard had a hit **Move It**, backed by The Drifters who later changed their name to The Shadows.

DECEMBER **It's Only Make Believe** peaked at No 1 on Christmas Day and Conway Twitty stayed at the top for five weeks.

POPULAR MUSIC

Elvis Presley had the most top 10 entries in 1958, with five, and all of them peaking within the top three. In January, **Jailhouse Rock** became the first-ever record to debut at No1 in the UK and went on to become the year's best-selling single.

The 1957 Christmas No1, **Mary's Boy Child** by Harry Belafonte stayed at No1 for two weeks in January.

JANUARY **Great Balls of Fire** was the first new No1 of the year for Jerry Lee Lewis.

FEBRUARY Pat Boone took **April Love** to No 7 in the charts. Written as the theme song for the film of the same name, starring Pat Boone, it was nominated for an Oscar for Best Music but lost out to **All the Way** by Frank Sinatra.

Doctors and scientists were beginning to gather evidence of the link between smoking and lung cancer and that it was harmful to your health, but in 1958 it was still promoted as a 'healthy', 'social' and 'fun' activity.

1964 THE YEAR

In 1964 Britain was engulfed in Beatlemania; mini-skirts were on the rise; Mods and Rockers took to fighting at the seaside and it was the year when The Great Train Robbers were jailed.

In October, thirteen years of Tory rule ended when Harold Wilson was elected Labour Prime Minister and in America, anti-Vietnam war protests were increasing.

The Forth Road Bridge opened; Winston Churchill retired and Radio Caroline, the 'pirate radio station' began broadcasting from a ship just outside UK territorial waters off Suffolk.

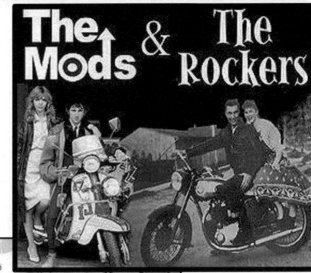

BUTLIN'S HOLIDAY CAMP SKEGNESS
IT'S QUICKER BY RAIL

Your holiday was still likely to be taken in England.

Holiday camps such as Butlins with their 'Red Coats' offered hours of fun, coaches could take you to the seaside and owning a caravan was becoming popular too. If you ate out, fish and chips was the most usual but Chinese restaurants were on the increase and teenagers loved the 'Wimpey Bar' for burgers.

CHILDREN AT ELEVEN

Age eleven was a milestone year for children. They went from being the 'king-pins' at primary school to 'the newcomers', either at Grammar School if they'd passed the 11+ exam or Secondary Modern if not. It was the start of growing up but at home there was still plenty of fun. Bikes and roller skates kept you out of the house; boys took to 'action figures' including 'GI Joe' and girls the Tiny Tears dolls. BBC aired the first **Top of the Pops** and BBC 2 started.

HOW MUCH DID IT COST?

The Average Pay:	£915 (£18 p.w)
The Average House:	£3,092
Loaf of White Bread:	1s 2d (6p)
Pint of Milk:	9d (4p)
Pint of Beer:	2s 3d (11p)
Gallon of Petrol:	5s 1p (25p)
12mnths Road Tax	£15
Newspapers:	3d - 9d (1p - 3)p
To post a letter in UK:	3d (1p)
TV Licence	£5 Black & White

POPULAR MUSIC

For the second successive year, The Beatles had the biggest-selling single of the year with **Can't Buy Me Love**. It spent three weeks at No1.

The group had a total of five top 10 entries, including two No1's from 1963, **She Loves You** and **I Want to Hold Your Hand** plus their fifth and sixth No1's **A Hard Day's Night** and **I Feel Fine**.

JANUARY **Glad All Over** by the Dave Clark Five was their first No1 hit and knocked the Beatles **I Want to Hold Your Hand** off the top spot.

FEBRUARY Bacharach and David wrote **Anyone Who Had a Heart** for Dionne Warwick but her version lost out to Cilla Black's in the UK, which stayed at No1 for three weeks

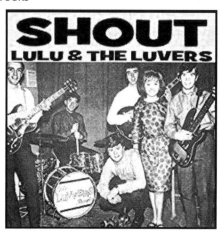

JUNE Scottish singer Lulu has her debut No1 hit with the Isley Brothers' 1959 hit, **Shout**.

JULY **A Hard Day's Night** by the Beatles featured on the soundtrack of their first feature film. The song topped the charts in both the UK and US.

OCTOBER Bare foot Sandie Shaw had her first No1 with **Always Something There to Remind Me**. Written by Bacharach and David, it had previously been 'demoed' by Dionne Warwick.

NOVEMBER **Little Red Rooster** by The Rolling Stones became the first blues standard to reach No1 but within a week Gene Pitney took the top spot with **I'm Gonna be Strong**.

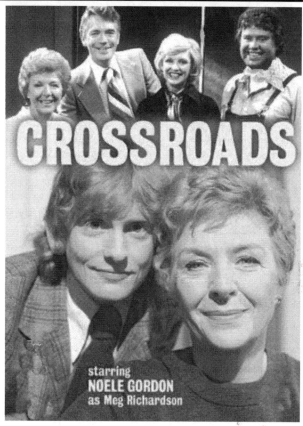

The daily soap opera **Crossroads** began in 1964. Set in a fictional motel in the Midlands the programme became the byword for cheap production values and had huge negative criticism – but despite this, it was loved by millions of regular fans.

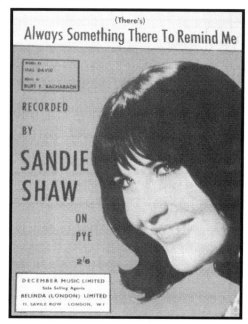

1969 The Year

WOODSTOCK
MUSIC AND ARTS FAIR

JIMI HENDRIX   JANIS JOPLIN

♪ AUGUST 15-16-17 - 1969 ♪
THREE DAY PEACE AND MUSIC FESTIVAL

★ FRIDAY THE 15th - Joan Baez, Arlo Guthrie, Richie
Havens, Sly & The Family Stone, Tim Hardin,
Nick Benes, Sha Na Na

★ SATURDAY THE 16th - Canned Heat, Creedence
Clearwater, Melanie, Grateful Dead, Janis Joplin
Jefferson Airplane, Incredible String Band, Santana
The Who, Paul Buttrfield, Keef Hartley

★ SUNDAY THE 17th - The Band, Crosby Stills Nash
and Young, Ten Years After, Blood Sweat & Tears
Joe Cocker, Jimi Hendrix, Mountain, Keef Hartley

AQUARIAN EXPOSITION
WHITE LAKE, NEW YORK

In 1969 Concord flew for the first time; the fifty pence piece arrived and there was an all-encompassing excitement of Apollo 11 and Neil Armstrong becoming the 'First Man on the Moon'.

Those left on the ground wanted to 'Make Love not War' and thirty-two acts performed to a crowd of more than 400,000, in sporadic rain, on a dairy farm in New York at the Woodstock music festival.

The nation's girls cried as the Beatles performed together for the last time on a London rooftop.

Young people were influenced by the political climate, they demonstrated in the streets against the Vietnam War, for civil rights and to 'Ban the Bomb'. Outdoor music festivals sprang up all over the country and thousands of, usually mud-caked, teenagers gathered to listen to their favourite artists.

LIFE AT SIXTEEN

Sixteen in 1969, you might have left school a year ago; could join the army; legally buy and smoke cigarettes; pubs were only open lunchtimes and evenings, but you couldn't have a beer unless an "adult" over 18 had bought it for you and you were eating a meal.

Fashion was being set by hippies and rock and roll groups. Psychedelic, tie-dye shirts, long hair and beards were commonplace. Miniskirts and brightly coloured and patterned tunics with flowing long skirts dominated fashion

Eating out was becoming more affordable and with the rise in immigrants from Asia, Chinese and Indian restaurants were springing up and their food became so popular that Vesta brought out their first 'foreign convenience' foods, the Vesta Curries and Vesta Chow Mein. Lager was invented – seemingly 'made for' the spicy food.

How Much Did It Cost?

The Average Pay:	£936 (£18 p.w)
The Average House:	£4201
Loaf of White Bread:	1s 8d (8p)
Pint of Milk:	2s 9d (13p)
Pint of Beer:	2s 9d (14p)
12mnths Road Tax	£25
Gallon of Petrol:	6s 6d (33p)
Newspapers:	5d - 1s (2-5p)
To post a letter in UK:	5d (2p)
TV Licence	£6 Black & White £11 Colour

YOU WERE SIXTEEN

APRIL **I Heard It Through the Grapevine** by Marvin Gaye went to No1 for three weeks and became the biggest hit single on the Motown label.

JULY **Honky Tonk Women** sung by The Rolling Stones topped the charts both in the UK and the US.

On July 20, 1969, Neil Armstrong became the first human to step on the moon. He and his co-astronaut Buzz Aldrin stayed for three hours collecting samples of rocks and left the 'Stars and Stripes' flying there.

POPULAR MUSIC

John Lennon had four UK top 10 singles in 1969, the most of any artist this year. Three of these were as part of The Beatles, **Get Back** and **The Ballad of John and Yoko** topped the charts.

The controversial **Je t'aime… moi non plus** was written in 1967 for Brigitte Bardot but Serge Gainsbourg and Jane Birkin reached number 1 in the UK in October. It was banned in several countries due to its overtly sexual content.

MARCH **Where Do You Go To (My Lovely)?** by Peter Sarstedt is a song about a fictional girl named Marie-Claire who grows up in the backstreets of Naples, becomes a member of the jet-set and goes on to live in Paris. It stayed at No1 for four weeks.

AUGUST Creedence Clearwater Revival had two UK top 10 hits this year, including **Bad Moon Rising** which spent three weeks at No1.

OCTOBER The Archies, a fictional American rock band that featured in media produced by, and related to, Archie Comics, took the bubblegum pop genre, **Sugar Sugar,** to No1 for eight weeks.

NOVEMBER **Yester-Me, Yester-You, Yesterday** reaches No2 in the charts and is Stevie Wonder's biggest UK hit at that time

1974 THE YEAR

1974 was a grim year for Britain economically, starting off with a 3-day week to conserve electricity, a 50mph speed limit on all roads and television was required to close down at 10.30 every evening. However, there was much to enjoy, the huge expansion of package holidays, particularly for destinations such as Torremolinos and Benidorm in Spain, meant families could forget their woes for a fortnight and enjoy the sun, sand and sangria. Abba won the Eurovision with **Waterloo** and all youngsters seemed to want to be Kung Fu fighting.

LOW PRICES GUARANTEED

Package tours to sunny, warm and cheap holiday destinations were very popular. Companies such as Thompson, Horizon, Global and Clarksons all used chartered planes to fly families to booming resorts Once there, holiday makers found that in addition to the sun and sand, food and drink was much cheaper than in the UK and this led to the rapid decline in UK seaside resorts and boom in once sleepy fishing villages such as Benidorm.

Kentucky Fried Chicken and Wimpey Bars were already established in Britain and when MacDonald's, serving hamburgers and French fries opened their first restaurant in London in 1974, the trend was sealed for fast food. Eating out became fun and fried food fast became a favourite. At home, the friendly Martians were encouraging everyone to eat Smash not Mash!

THE TERRACOTTA ARMY

The Terracotta Army of Qin Shi Huang, thousands of life-size clay models of soldiers, horses and chariots, was discovered at Xi'an in China.

The figures, dating from approximately the late third century BC eventually amounted to more than 8,000 soldiers, 130 chariots with 520 horses, and 150 cavalry horses, plus other terracotta non-military figures including officials, acrobats, strongmen, and musicians.

HOW MUCH DID IT COST?

The Average Pay:	£2,500 (£48 p.w)
The Average House:	£10,000
Loaf of White Bread:	14p
Pint of Milk:	4p
Pint of Beer:	22p
Gallon of Petrol:	50p
12mnths Road Tax	£25
Newspapers:	43p - 8p
To post a letter in UK:	4.5p
TV Licence	£7 Black & White £12 Colour

YOU WERE 21

POPULAR MUSIC

ABBA, Eric Clapton, Queen and Showaddywaddy were among the artists who had their first UK No 1 hit. The 1973 Christmas No1, **Merry Christmas Everybody** by Slade stayed at the top for two weeks in January.

Mud had the best-selling single of the year with **Tiger Feet** which spent four weeks at No1 and the glam-rock group had three other top 10's including the Christmas No1, **Lonely This Christmas.**

FEBRUARY The Wombles had four hits, **Wombling Song** No4, **Remember You're a Womble**, No3, **Banana Rock** No9 and **Wombling Merry Christmas** No2.

Popular TV programmes included: Are You Being Served?, The Benny Hill Show, Colditz, Dad's Army, and Doctor Who. The main soaps were Emmerdale (started 1972) and Coronation Street (1960). Radio's The Archers had started in 1951.

MARCH Paper Lace had the first of two top-ten singles this year with **Billy Don't Be a Hero**. It stayed at No1 for three weeks.

JUNE Charles Aznavour wrote **She** in English as the theme song for the TV series 'Seven Faces of Woman' and it became his only UK No1.

JULY The first Knebworth open air, rock and pop concert is held in England. Headlined by The Allman Brothers Band and the Doobie Brothers, only 60,000 fans attended.

NOVEMBER **Gonna Make You a Star,** was the first No1 for David Essex and the first of many top forty hits made by the singer who combined singing with an extensive acting career.

DECEMBER Barry White had two weeks at the top before Christmas with **You're the First, the Last, My Everything.**

15

1953

SPORTING HEADLINES

JANUARY Ken Rosewall won the **Australian Open** for his first grand slam title at just 18 years of age.

MARCH India finished their first **Cricket** tour of the West Indies, losing a five-test series 0–1 with four draws.

The **Rugby** Five Nations Championship series was won by England.

Canada did not participate in the **World Hockey Championships** held in Basel and Zurich, the government claiming it was not worth the expense. Sweden won their first World Championship title and their seventh European Championship title.

MAY In the **FA Cup** Final at Wembley, Stanley Matthews inspired Blackpool to come from 3–1 down against Bolton Wanderers, to win 4–3, and he claimed the trophy that had eluded him in two previous finals. Known as the 'Matthews Final', it was actually Stan Mortensen who scored the 'hat-trick'.

JULY Ben Hogan won **The Open** at Carnoustie and won 'The Triple Crown of Golf'. He was unable to enter—and possibly win—the PGA Championship to complete the Grand Slam, because it overlapped **The Open.**

AUGUST Maureen Connolly (USA) became the first woman to win the **Grand Slam** in tennis. The Australian Open, the French Open, Wimbledon and the US Open.

SEPTEMBER Italian Alberto Ascari won the **F1 Driver's championships** for the second consecutive time, driving a Ferrari on both occasions.

In New York City, Rocky Marciano retained his World Heavyweight **Boxing** title with a technical knockout over Roland La Starza in the 11th round.

OCTOBER The golf **Ryder Cup Matches** were held at Wentworth, Virginia Water where the United States team won its sixth consecutive competition by a score of 6½ to 5½ points.

SPORTING EVENTS

THE CORONATION DERBY

Edmund Hillary had reached the summit of Everest, the Queen had been crowned on Tuesday and her horse, 'Aureole', a beautiful Chestnut with a white blaze down his face, ridden by Harry Carr was hoping to win the Derby at Epsom for her on Saturday. The Coronation Honours List had been announced with a knighthood for Gordon Richards, Britain's champion Flat jockey for nearly three decades, who was to ride an arch-rival, 'Pinza'. By the end of the afternoon of June 6th, Richards, who had been trying since 1924, had won his first Derby, beating the Queen's horse into second place. It was his 28th and last attempt to claim racing's Holy Grail.

Richards had first been champion jockey in 1925 aged 21 but missed the following year as he was ill with tuberculosis. A broken leg in 1941 and being beaten 'fair and square' by Freddie Fox, with a single win, in 1930, meant he had been champion jockey 26 times, but he was jinxed by the Derby.

The only accusation levelled at Richards was that he sometimes chose the wrong horse when offered the choice for the big race. Apart from that he was blameless. Every horse he ever rode - and there were 21,834 in his extraordinary career - got a committed ride. "He never lost a race that he should have won," was the punters' verdict.

His luck changed in 1952 when riding out at Newmarket Heath, he was 'raced' by a large bay colt and left behind. He teamed up with 'Pinza', and eventually came the Coronation Derby. 'Aureole' was just one competitor in a very strong field of 27. 'Premonition' and 'Pinza' started as 5-1 joint favourites, with 'Aureole' at 9-1, but from the off, Richards in the peacock blue and gold hoops of Sir Victor Sassoon made it all look easy. In one brief, whirling harlequinade of galloping hooves, streaming colours, shouting jockeys, with seven furlongs to go, 'Pinza' accelerated towards the roar of the grandstand and won by four lengths.

1953

THE CRUCIBLE AND McCARTHY

Arthur Miller's play 'The Crucible' was first performed on Broadway in January. It is set in Salem, Massachusetts, during the 1692 Salem witch trials. The small community of Salem is stirred into madness by superstition, paranoia and malice and is a savage attack on the evils of mindless persecution and the terrifying power of false accusations.

Miller drew a chilling parallel with Senator Joseph McCarthy's anti-communist purges of the 50's. McCarthy instigated a series of investigations and hearings to expose supposed communist infiltration of various areas of the US government, the CIA and the State Department and questioned innumerable witnesses about their suspected communist affiliations. Although he failed to make a plausible case against anyone, his accusations drove some persons out of their jobs and brought popular condemnation to others.

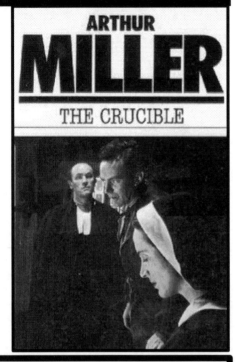

ARTHUR **MILLER**
THE CRUCIBLE

THE COFFEE REVOLUTION

Gina Lollobrigida opened the 'Moka Bar', the first coffee house in London to install the revolutionary Gaggia espresso machine. Strong black espresso and frothy milk soon became de rigueur in all coffee bars. Teenagers began to 'exist' in the fifties, they had disposable income to spend and time to socialise, all that was missing were places to gather.

Too young to drink in pubs, the answer for many of them was the new espresso bar especially as, there, they could listen to the latest music on the jukebox. The drink of choice was coffee - Italian and served from the gurgling monster Gaggia, it was combined with steamed-milk foam and served in glass cups. The height of 'continental sophistication' Moka, with its bright, formica covered tables, was soon serving over a thousand cups of coffee a day.

Moka Bar

GAGGIA *Espresso Coffee Machines*

The Soho Coffee Bar Boom

CULTURAL EVENTS

FONTEYN THE TOAST OF THE TOWN

In January, Royal ballerina Margot Fonteyn appeared on American television in Ed Sullivan's, 'Toast of the Town', which ran every Sunday night and featured virtually every type of entertainment from classical musicians and opera singers to popular recording artists, comedians and even circus acts. The show enjoyed phenomenal popularity in the '50s and the appearance of Margot Fonteyn, a star Prima Ballerina, is credited with increasing the popularity of not only ballet, but all dance, in the United States.

It was on this American tour that she was suddenly reacquainted with Roberto 'Tito' Arias, with whom she had spent time at Cambridge, when he surprised her with a visit to her dressing room after a performance of 'Sleeping Beauty'. Arias was now a politician and Panamanian delegate to the UN and they eventually married.

LONDON TO BRIGHTON - AND BACK

The gentle comedy, 'Genevieve', must have seemed pleasantly nostalgic even in the '50s. It featured the antics of two obsessive enthusiasts on the annual London to Brighton vintage car rally. Starring John Gregson, Dinah Sheridan, Kenneth More, Kay Kendall and a St Bernard, 'Genevieve' breaks down, jokes are made at its expense, a boastful wager is made, and the result - a return race to

London. The musical score, composed and performed by American harmonica player Larry Adler, was nominated for an Oscar but his name was originally removed from the credits in the US. During the McCarthy era he was accused of being a communist and put on the Hollywood Blacklist. Adler moved to the UK in 1951 and settled in London.

1953

THE SECRET OF LIFE REVEALED

In February, two molecular scientists from Cambridge University James D. Watson and Francis Crick announced they had determined the double-helix structure of DNA, the molecule containing human genes. Watson claimed that Crick announced the discovery by walking into the nearby Eagle Pub and blurting out *'we have found the secret of life.'* The truth wasn't that different, they had solved the mystery of how genetic instructions were held inside organisms and passed from generation to generation.

Among the developments that followed directly from this discovery, are pre-natal screening for disease genes; genetically engineered foods; the ability to identify human remains; the rational design of treatments for diseases such as AIDS and the accurate testing of physical evidence in order to convict or exonerate criminals.

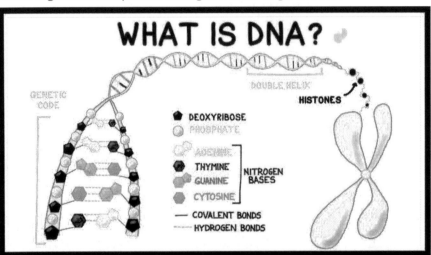

THE BLACK BOX FLIGHT RECORDER

This invention by an Australian, David Warren, has saved many lives since it was introduced in 1953. Before then, the cause of most plane crashes, unless there was a surviving pilot, remained unknown, and working as a researcher at an Aeronautical Laboratory in Melbourne, Warren realised that if there was a device in the cockpit that recorded the pilot's voice and read instruments, the information gathered could reveal the cause of the crash and could possibly prevent subsequent ones.

His first device called the Flight Memory Unit could record about four hours of voice and certain parameters but was rejected on grounds of privacy by the Australian aviation community. Luckily, British officials accepted it, production of the devices in fireproof containers, began and it was taken up by airlines around the world. Some years later it was made compulsory for Australian airlines.

SCIENCE AND NATURE

SALK'S POLIO VACCINE

Polio or infantile paralysis is a highly infectious disease, mostly affecting young children, that attacks the nervous system, and can lead to paralysis and in some cases death. In 1952, it killed over 3,000 people in New York. Many who survived faced leg braces, crutches or wheelchairs and some were confined to an 'iron lung', an artificial respirator invented specifically for polio patients.

Whilst working as the head of the Virus Research Lab at the University of Pittsburgh, Jonas Salk, an American doctor discovered and perfected the first safe, effective, vaccine against polio.

After preliminary tests on laboratory animals, Salk tested his vaccine on children and nearly 2 million young 'polio pioneers' were injected in 1952/53. In 1953, Salk tested the still-experimental vaccine on himself, his wife and sons.

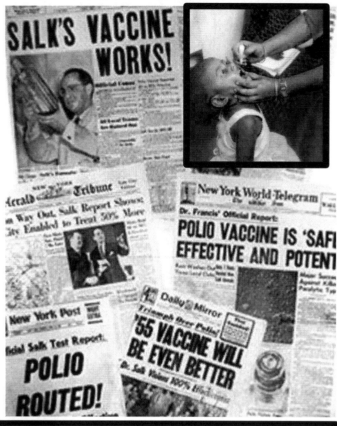

CATATUMBO LIGHTNING

In Venezuela, where the mouth of the Catatumbo River meets Lake Maracaibo, a unique and impressive natural phenomenon, known as the 'Catatumbo lightning occurs. On about 260 storm days a year, the night sky is lit up for nine hours at a time, with lightning striking about 28 times per minute. The spectacle can be seen from as much as 400 kilometres away.

The exact reason is not known but one theory is that winds blowing across Lake Maracaibo and the surrounding swampy plains give rise to warm, wet air masses which meet the mountains that enclose the plain. The Catatumbo lightning has been seen for centuries and locals are alarmed when it stops, even if for a while, as it is such a regular part of their daily life.

1953 LIFESTYLES OF

During 1953 very few people had a television and the wireless reigned supreme. Daytime programmes were for wives, mothers and their children. 'Workers Playtime' continued to "come to you from a factory somewhere in England" and singers were interspersed with the major comedians of the day, Arthur Askey, Tommy Trinder, Charlie Chester and Ted Ray.

Music was important, with 'Music while you work' and 'Housewives Choice'. Soap operas gripped us, 'Mrs Dale's Diary' and 'The Archers'. Sunday lunchtimes meant 'Two-Way Family Favourites', music and messages for the troops in Germany. On Saturday evening we could "Stop the roar of London's mighty traffic" and listen to 'In Town Tonight', and the children weren't forgotten, they had 'Listen with Mother', Children's Hour 'Children's Favourites' with Uncle Mac.

Sweet rationing ended in 1953 and happy children with a few pennies pocket money could choose sweeties from the rows of jars on the shelves. Four blackjacks or fruit salads for a penny, a Barratt's Sherbet Fountain with a stick of liquorice in it, raspberry drops, dolly mixture or toffees. You could 'smoke' a sweet cigarette whilst reading Dan Dare's adventures in Eagle or laugh with Radio Fun, Beano and Dandy comics.

The drabness of the war years gave way by 1953 to an age of colour and plastic in the home. Textile restrictions had been lifted and consumers were eager for new brightly patterned curtains and upholstery, and in the kitchen there were new coloured plastic goods.

G Plan furniture arrived. This new modular system was a range of modern furniture for the entire house which could be bought piece-by-piece according to budgets and individual room arrangements.

In 1953 the nuclear family was the norm, father out at work and mother busy with the housework. Less than 10% of households had a refrigerator, meat was stored in a wire mesh 'safe' in the larder,

vegetables wilted on a rack and shopping was done daily. It was the time of spam fritters, salmon sandwiches, tinned fruit with evaporated milk and ham salad for high tea on Sundays. Salad in the summer consisted of round lettuce, cucumber and tomatoes, and the only dressing available was Heinz Salad Cream, olive oil only came in tiny bottles from the chemist for your ears!

Many housewives wanted a Kenwood Chef to make baking and food preparation easier. And these new domestic inventions coincided with an upsurge in 'do-it-yourself' or DIY from the mid-1950s. The nation that had adopted a 'make do and mend' attitude during wartime privations took very readily to the idea of improving their homes themselves.

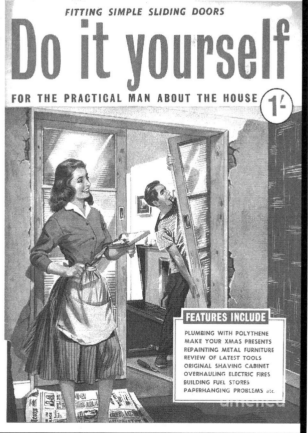

FITTING SIMPLE SLIDING DOORS

Do it yourself

FOR THE PRACTICAL MAN ABOUT THE HOUSE 1/-

FEATURES INCLUDE

PLUMBING WITH POLYTHENE
MAKE YOUR XMAS PRESENTS
REPAINTING METAL FURNITURE
REVIEW OF LATEST TOOLS
ORIGINAL SHAVING CABINET
OVERHAULING ELECTRIC FIRES
BUILDING FUEL STORES
PAPERHANGING PROBLEMS etc.

23

JANUARY 1ST - 7TH 1953

IN THE NEWS

Thursday 1   **"Trade Agreement Signed with Argentina"** The Ministry of Food states that if the estimates of meat supplies based on this agreement are realised, the amount of meat available in Britain in 1953 should be the largest since the war.

Friday 2   **"French Prospect in Viet Nam"** France and Viet Nam face a doubtful prospect in Indochina. The present positions were intended to be only temporary and the deadlock in fighting rebels is proof that neither side has won serious advantages in the field.

Saturday 3   **"Traders Move on Higher Purchase"** Leaders of the principal retail furniture trade associations agreed a minimum deposit of 10 % on hire-purchase agreements for household furniture, down from 12½%, and a maximum period of two years' credit.

Sunday 4   **"Two More Settlers Killed"** Two more British settlers in Kenya have been murdered by armed Kikuyu who raided a farm in the Thomson's Falls district. Aircraft and troops were taking part in the search for the gang responsible.

Monday 5   **"Demands for Tougher Action Against Mau Mau"** A loyal Kikuyu chief was murdered in the hospital where he was recovering from his wounds from an earlier ambush.

Tuesday 6   **"52 Killed in Belfast Air Crash"** A BEA aircraft crashed at Nutt's Corner airport, Belfast and 27 people were killed. There were eight survivors.

Wednesday 7   **"George Cross for Sergeant Fairfax"** The hero of the roof-top gun battle in which PC Miles was killed by Christopher Craig, is the first Met Police Officer to be awarded the George Cross.

HERE IN BRITAIN

"Junk for St Paul's Christmas Tree"

Canon Collins, preaching in St. Paul's Cathedral, complained as he dangled a pair of socks over the pulpit and said, *"Who would want an elderly person to receive this pair of socks? They were handed in unwashed and so worn and darned that they would hardly bear another stitch of wool on them.*

Although many beautiful gifts have been received, too much rubbish has been handed in by people who think that any old junk would do - because it was for poor children and poor old people who cannot afford to buy the nice things of this world."

AROUND THE WORLD

"Coronation TV"

Plans to televise the Coronation of Queen Elizabeth direct to New York from London were completed this week. Hush-hush research work has been going on for six months and the proposal is a chain of transmitting and receiving stations from New York to the Shetlands, via Canada and the coasts of Labrador, Greenland and Iceland. Between Iceland and Scotland will be small ships carrying aerials, and experiments prove that pictures can be transmitted over such enormous distances with perfect clarity. If agreed, work can begin almost immediately on the construction of hundreds of elevated TV towers.

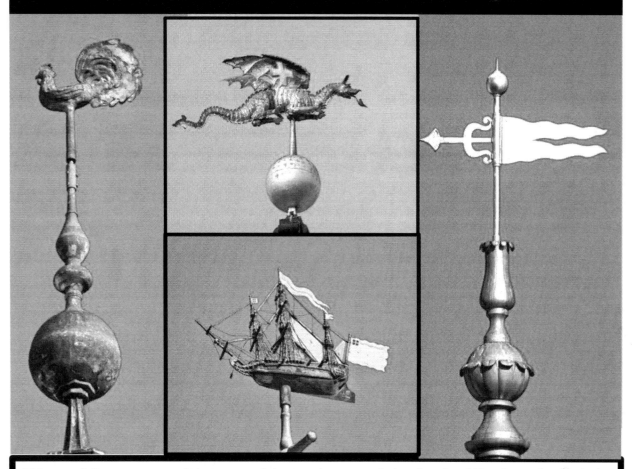

This month it was suggested that many of the weather vanes in London should be cleaned and oiled in time for the Coronation. The capital still has many weather vanes, but most are plain arrows on church steeples, usually with a rather wide vane (or banner) as the tail to catch the wind. Some churches vanes carry the emblem of the saint to whom they are dedicated, just as St. Peter-upon-Cornhill has keys as its design.

The tiny City church of St. Ethelburga in Bishopsgate has one of London's few remaining weathercocks, the cock itself forming the whole of one side of the vane, the other side being a banner with the date 1675. In Bishopsgate, above St. Helen's Place, the weather vane is in the form of a beaver and above the Worshipful Company of Leather sellers there is a fine antlered head. In Threadneedle Street, where the 'Old Lady' has no weather vane, is one of the City's most imposing, the giant grasshopper on the Royal Exchange. The weather vane of St. Michael, Queenhithe, a City church demolished in the last century, is now on a building near the site of the church and is in the form of a sailing ship. In former times its hull was reputed to hold a bushel of grain in token of the trade in corn carried on at Queenhithe.

Another ship in full sail can be seen on a building near London Bridge and close beside it, is a weather vane that takes the form of a multi-shafted arrow with a single head. From London Bridge you can see the huge fish that make the vanes for Billingsgate Market. Leadenhall Market has smaller twin cock pheasants. The Tower of London has many banners that turn 'with the wind, and the unattractive outposts of Cannon Street station on each of which is a plain arrow type of weather vane that has become a favourite roosting-place for starlings.

JANUARY 8TH - 14TH 1953

IN THE NEWS

Thursday 8 "Bombers Collision with Car" A four-engine Lincoln bomber coming into land at RAF Lindholme near Doncaster, hit the roof of a car travelling on the main road and killed the woman driver.

Friday 9 "Mr Churchill in America" The Prime Minister finished his visit in Washington where he had a 'friendly, social' meeting with President Truman. He leaves for his holiday in Jamaica today.

Saturday 10 "We Must Get More or – Crisis" This was the grim warning given to miners by the Chairman of the Coal Board. He emphasised the need to maintain a steady flow of coal exports which, in turn, required an improvement in production.

Sunday 11 "Crossings into West Berlin Reduced Again" Russian soldiers and east German police have used barbed wire to close points between west Berlin and the Russian zone, leaving only one pedestrian and five road crossings.

Monday 12 "£3,000 Taken in Hold Up at Inn" Scotland Yard issued the description of four young men "of smart appearance" after an armed hold-up at the 'Prospect of Whitby' at Wapping. They wore light coloured raincoats, with red scarves over their faces.

Tuesday 13 "New Threat as Talks Re-Open" As critical talks re-opened between Britain and Egypt in Cairo, Egypt's Premier, General Naguib, told cheering students, "We will continue our struggle until not one foreign soldier remains on Egyptian soil."

Wednesday 14 "One Penny Increase in Meat Ration" As a result of the Anglo-Argentine trade agreement, the meat ration is to be increased from 1s 8d to 1s 9d a week.

HERE IN BRITAIN

"Rum Reason to Keep Dates"

Navy rum is such very strong stuff that it can be lethal in large quantities so now every RN ship keeps a birthday book and when a man's birthday comes round, his shipmates are told 'Don't give him your rum ration'. During the war, the rum ration killed young twins, they were found to have drunk three pints of rum each, given it by their shipmates to celebrate.

Rum is not issued to anyone under the age of twenty. Junior ratings are given a diluted rum but senior men such as petty officers are given it neat and can water it themselves if they wish.

AROUND THE WORLD

"Ice From Above"

Wide areas of the north-eastern states were ice-bound over the weekend in the worst storm of the winter. Steady rain froze as it fell, transforming roads into sheets of ice, obscuring the windscreens of motor-vehicles, and giving a shimmering beauty to the wintry woodlands.

Power cables and telephone lines were breaking and in New York City some of the taller skyscrapers created their own hazard of falling icicles. The street in which the Chrysler Building is situated had to be closed because of this danger.

BETTER BRIGHTER CLOTHES

The London winter sales are in full swing and bargain hunters are showing a much bigger demand for the more expensive clothes which have been marked down than for the clothes being sold at rock-bottom prices. Women are wanting more glamorous clothes, especially furs, in preparation for coronation year parties. Beaver lamb coats have been considered the best bargains, costing £24 or even less, and there have been more available than for many years. For those who could not afford so much, the stylish coats of rabbit fur, or 'coney' as the trade likes it to be called, selling at about £17 and jackets costing £12 have been the favourites - rabbit skin coats are free of tax if they cost less than £12 10s. There has been a demand also for fox capes costing £6 and some musquash coats were reduced from £125 to 69 guineas. Whilst in one shop fur and fur-trimmed coats were the best sellers, nothing rivalled the 100 pairs of coloured slacks which cost 2s 6d (12p) and were sold in 30 minutes and the fog in December soiled many articles of women's clothing on display and these, including expensive dresses and coats, have been sold at greatly reduced prices.

This year the 'male sale' has also found unexpected popularity. The demand for suits and overcoats, even if the colours are no less drab than wartime, shows a distinct preference for the better-quality materials. A Piccadilly shop reported that good quality overcoats of the beltless variety, sports clothes and shirts were selling the quickest. That there is a secret longing for more colour in this coronation year is indicated by the increased sale of fancy waistcoats in shops where they have been spurned in the past and the modern American bow tie and the gaily spotted Churchillian version seem to appeal to the converted.

JANUARY 15ᵀᴴ - 21ˢᵀ 1953

IN THE NEWS

Thursday 15 **"Cheaper Air Travel for Spring"** British European Airways tourist services, to be introduced throughout its Continental network on April 1, will be operated at fares averaging 20% below those for current standard services.

Friday 16 **"Nazi Power Bid is Smashed"** In a dramatic midnight swoop on luxury homes in west Germany, the British authorities arrested seven ringleaders of a group of former leading Nazis found to be infiltrating the German political parties.

Saturday 17 **"Daimler Dismissals"** 150 men are to be dismissed at Coventry, after the Chancellor's ambiguous statement on car purchase tax earlier this year, had such an effect on sales that the production of some models has stopped.

Sunday 18 **"Mr & Mrs Churchill in Jamaica"** Thousands of Jamaicans cheered as they drove in an open car through the main streets and received the "freedom of the city of Kingston". The couple are spending a fortnight's holiday on the island.

Monday 19 **"Nazism Gains Ground"** A US High Commission survey provides proof of the growth of Nazism, especially within the Free Democratic Party. It offers additional justification of the action taken in the British zone in putting leading Nazis under lock and key.

Tuesday 20 **"Inauguration of New President"** President Dwight (Ike) Eisenhower was sworn in at a ceremony in Washington.

Wednesday 21 **"Car Covenants Ending"** The last British car was freed from the covenant which prohibited resale for 12 months after purchase. The restriction had already been withdrawn from many models, but still applied to the Austin A30, Morris Minor, Ford Anglia and Prefect, and the Vauxhall Wyvern and Velox.

HERE IN BRITAIN

"Jobs for the Boys"

Boys leaving school or college should find choosing a suitable career easier than before the war. Not only are there more jobs, but there are fewer boys to fill them. The 15 to 18 age-group ready for employment is only two-thirds of its size in 1938 and next year it will be smaller still. After that the age-group will increase, as will competition for jobs, but the 1938 level will not be reached again until 1960-61. Career masters tend to be more knowledgeable now and the Youth Employment Service extended to include industrial psychology, is a useful long stop for the 'boy without a clue'.

AROUND THE WORLD

"A New President"

In Washington, General 'Ike' Eisenhower was sworn in as the thirty-fourth President of the United States. He took the oath with his hand on two Bibles, one of which was used by George Washington when he became the first President in 1789. After the inaugural address the President lead a huge procession from the Capitol to the White House. In a break with tradition, he wore a homburg instead of a silk hat, *'in which sartorial originality all the assembled dignitaries followed suit'*, much to the regret of the Washington stores who had laid in a stock of silk hats.

DELAYS ON THE MOTORWAYS

Early roads followed the historic pack horse routes.

In the 1960s many roads were narrow and windy.

The United Kingdom in 1963, has the densest traffic of any country in the world with more than 4,600,000 vehicles on its 184,837 miles of road. The resulting traffic jams and delays are exacerbated by a road system that is widely the same as it was before the coming of the motor vehicle. Even some major roads tend to have a width sufficient only for two wagons to pass, two oxherds to make their goads – a long stick with a pointed end used for prodding the animals - touch across the road, or 16 armed knights to ride side by side.

After the war the Government reviewed 8,249 miles of trunk roads and decided that they were both inefficient and dangerous for much of their length because of their *inferior and irregular widths, steep gradients, frequent intersections, blind corners, long stretches of built-up frontages and weak bridges.* Nearly 1,400 miles of the trunk roads were found to be subject to a 30mph speed limit, they had more than 100 railway level-crossings and in general, were in a poor state of repair because maintenance had been neglected during the war. It was accepted that approximately 450 miles of trunk roads which could not be made fit for modern traffic without excessive cost should be relieved by the construction of a limited number of motorways and others would be made into two-lane carriageways and their bridges strengthened.

The Special Roads Act of 1949 gave the green light for construction, surveys and planning have been carried out but as yet, there are no motorways and the development and improvement of trunk roads has not started. It has been estimated that by 1960 the number of vehicles on our roads might be as many as 6,500,000 and by 1970 it might even reach nine million. Drastic measures are needed.

JANUARY 22ND - 28TH 1953

IN THE NEWS

Thursday 22   **"Controls on Cereals Removed"** Subsidies and restrictions on type of flour will go, leaving a choice of whiter bread, not subject to price control, and the present national loaf, the price of which will remain unchanged.

Friday 23   **"Deadlock in Miners' Pay Talks"** After reaching deadlock in their wages talks with the National Coal Board, the miners' leaders are to seek to appeal to the Government. Until then, they will refuse the board's latest offer and stop Saturday working.

Saturday 24   **"Gen. Naguib on Next Task"** The Egyptian Prime Minister said that *"having swept away the corrupt politicians who had hampered Egyptian unity, divided them from their Sudanese brothers and helped the British occupation to continue, the task was now to get rid of the last traces of British imperialism"*.

Sunday 25   **"Empress of Canada Ablaze"** Fire broke out in the £5m Canadian Pacific liner 'Empress of Canada'. About 200 firemen battled for 9 hours to save her but, blazing from end to end, she heeled over and sank.

Monday 26   **"Sunshine Brings Out the Motorists"** Several hours of sunshine brought out the day trippers equal to that on a spring Sunday. On the main London to Portsmouth road, some 1,400 vehicles an hour were passing through Cobham at 4pm.

Tuesday 27   **"Emergency Council Set Up in Kenya"** Following another murder of an English family by the Mau Mau last weekend, the former British Military Governor in Berlin is to become the personal staff officer to the Governor of Kenya for action against terrorists.

Wednesday 28   **"Derek Bentley Hanged for Murder"** Teenager Derek Bentley was executed at Wandsworth Prison in London for his part in the murder of PC Sidney Miles.

HERE IN BRITAIN
"The Rising Price of a Porter's Hat"

Billingsgate fish porters' retaining fee was raised from £2 5s to £2 15s a week. Porters' special hats cost 30s £1.50) in 1939 but now cost £6. 'Pushers-up' used by porters to help push their barrows uphill could be hired for 2d, now 6d (2p) each. The man they took round to heave the packages on their heads charged 6d a round and now, 2s (10p). 'Bobbin charges', 70% of a porter's total earnings, are paid by the customer for carrying the fish; 'shoring-in' money is paid by the merchant to his porters for carrying fish and 'foreign fish', 2d a stone, paid by the merchant on all foreign fish handled.

AROUND THE WORLD
"Fighting the Waves"

Holland's perennial struggle against the sea is providing more useful land. Some of the latest achievement comes from 'in-dyking', or enclosure, of the Lauwerszee, a large inlet between the provinces of Friesland and Groningen, work which is closely connected with the greater project of draining the shallows between the Dutch Wadden Islands. The difficulty here is caused by constant silting up in places and the frequent movement of sand, which if and when it is drained, may make the task of laying down firm foundations problematic.

Australian big game fishermen, specialising in sharks of world record size, congregate at Streaky Bay, an inlet high up on the long sweep of the west coast of South Australia, washed by the Great Australian Bight. The latest catch is a monster of 2,372lb, named 'Barnacle Phyl' and Alfred Dean of Victoria had a great fight. The shark measured 15ft 11in and had a girth of 9ft 9in. Once it had taken the bait Mr Dean realised he had a champion on the line by the flurry of leaps, dives, and twists. The line was carried out about 350 yards, and Dean had to leave his chair and play the fish from the rigging. It took 95 minutes to pull in by the hands - the shark and the achievement was threatened by a second monster which kept circling his boat. The prize could have been lost by the cruising shark fouling the line, or even attacking and mutilating 'Barnacle Phyl'.

Last year, the new record holder landed a 2,333-pounder, just eclipsing the 2,225-pounder caught by the then Governor of South Australia and now Governor-General elect of New Zealand, Sir Willoughby Norrie.

The rivalry at Streaky Bay is widespread and exciting, inspired by the report that another shark, estimated to weigh 3,000lb, is in the vicinity. Distinguished by a big scar running from the gills, she is known as 'Barnacle Lil' and to land her would be a memorable feat. Mr Dean says he hooked her last year but had to let the line break. When hooked, most fish will circulate in different directions and when they are not pulling away from the boat the fisherman can take the opportunity to reel in some of the line. Eventually, if the fish tires and has not broken the line, they will be reeled in.

JAN 29TH - FEB 4TH 1953

IN THE NEWS

Thursday 29   **"Parachutists in Tree Tops"** Parachute troops have been used in Malaya, dropped purposely on to the treetops. The method, developed by the American Army, is safer than dropping troops on open ground.

Friday 30   **"200 RN Ships for Coronation Review"** Nearly 200 ships will take part in the Coronation review at Spithead on June 15. The Commonwealth will send ships and the Merchant Navy and fishing fleet will also be represented.

Saturday 31   **"Sundays Stay as They Are"** The Sunday Observance Bill seeking to legalise all games and sports which are now legal on weekdays and to permit by local option the Sunday opening of theatres, was soundly beaten in the Commons.

Sunday Feb 1   **"Floods: Thousands Homeless"** Hundreds of people living on the east coast of Britain have died in one of the worst storms ever recorded and hundreds more are missing.

Monday 2   **"130 Die in Ferry Disaster"** The Stranraer to Larne, Northern Ireland, car ferry has sunk in the Irish Sea in one of the worst gales in living memory, claiming the lives of more than 130 passengers and crew.

Tuesday 3   **"York Aircraft Missing"** A York transport aircraft belonging to the London firm Skyways is missing on a trooping flight, between the UK and Jamaica. It was carrying 33 passengers, including families, and a crew of six.

Wednesday 4   **"Floods Slowly Recede"** The battle goes on to close the breaches in the sea and river defences on the east coast between Kent and the mouth of the Humber. It is estimated that about 30,000 people have lost their homes.

HERE IN BRITAIN

"Biggest Peacetime Catastrophe"

Sheerness dockyard was completely flooded by the great tide and the frigate 'Berkeley Castle' and the submarine 'Sirdar', both capsized in the dock. The frigate ended on her beam ends with her mast snapped off close to the top. The 'Sirdar', in the next dock, was left on her port side surrounded by floating timber and broken scaffolding. The Sirdar, is easier to salvage, although much of her equipment, including nearly all her electrical gear, will have to be stripped from her hull first. The 'Berkeley Castle', 1,060 tons may have to be broken up in the dock.

AROUND THE WORLD

"Flood Havoc in Holland"

Holland declared a state of national emergency as the floods have left behind miles of dangerously weakened dykes. Although the first fears of the dunes north of the Hook of Holland letting through the sea seem have lessened, the hinterland of the port is deeply flooded; much of Rotterdam is under water and the city is approachable only from the north. The main road and railway from Belgium are cut by floods. In the maritime provinces of north and south Brabant and Zeeland the damage is most widespread of all. Evacuees in a constant stream are being taken to inland towns.

NORTH SEA FLOODS DROWN HUNDREDS

An intense depression caused gale force northerly winds to lash the east coast and break through flood defences from Yorkshire down to Kent. Combined with spring tides, the wind formed a fatal combination which claimed hundreds of lives and flooded thousands of homes on low-lying land here and in Belgium and The Netherlands.

The first fatalities on land were reported after 20ft (6m) waves crashed through flood defences in Lincolnshire and then, throughout the night, the high winds travelled down the east coast ripping through sea walls and claiming dozens of lives. Water was gushing through streets; thousands of homes were flooded, and many people were forced to spend the night on their rooftops waiting to be rescued by over-stretched emergency services. Counties worst affected were Yorkshire, Lincolnshire, Norfolk, Suffolk, Essex and Kent. On Canvey Island, Essex, nearly 100 bodies were recovered despite the police compelling the evacuation of 13,000-residents in dinghies and fishing boats to safety.

In the aftermath, the Queen and the Duke of Edinburgh, visited flood-damaged areas in west Norfolk whilst thousands of civilians and service men worked to rescue trapped families, some marooned for more than 36 hours. They had to be brought to safety, fed, and accommodated. The bodies of the dead had to be recovered. Gaps torn in sea defences and in riverbanks had to be sealed and embankments strengthened.

Electricity and gas supplies had to be brought back to normal, and the water mains protected from pollution. Eastern Command arranged to deliver six million sandbags to Army depots; searchlight units were sent to enable work to continue during the night; bulldozers and Army kitchens went to the scene. Civil Defence food convoys originally intended to meet war-time emergencies were dispatched from Cambridge and lorries took thousands of blankets to coastal towns where the homeless had been accommodated in schools, hotels, and private houses.

FEBRUARY 5TH - 11TH 1953

IN THE NEWS

Thursday 5   **"Fight to Save Thousands from Dutch Islands"** With stormy weather forecast, there is anxiety for some of the islands on which thousands of villagers are still marooned.

Friday 6   **"Flood Relief"** Contributions to the Lord Mayor of London's National Flood and Tempest Distress Fund included a gift of £A100,000 from the Government of Australia to be shared among victims equally in Holland and the UK.

Saturday 7   **"1s 6d a Week to House a Flood Victim"** The Government is to pay a lodging allowance of 1s 6d (7p) per person, and half that for a child, to householders who shelter a victim of the east coast floods.

Sunday 8   **"Birching Debate"** The House of Lords is to debate this week a Bill to restore birching. Although the Bill has a good measure of Conservative support there are no fewer than four motions for its rejection.

Monday 9   **"Six Lost in Lifeboat"** Five of the crew of seven on the lifeboat lost their lives at Fraserburgh, a fishing village 42 miles from Aberdeen, when it was caught by a big wave at the mouth of the harbour, and capsized.

Tuesday 10   **"A Common Market"** The common market for coal and iron ore and scrap for the six member countries of the European coal and steel community came into operation, six months after the treaty establishing the organisation came into force.

Wednesday 11   **"After the Floods, the Snow"** Ice and snow affected roads in all districts of England and Wales north of a line from Wells in Somerset to the Wash. Only eight counties were unaffected.

HERE IN BRITAIN

"Sweet Rationing Ends in Britain"

Children all over Britain took their pocket money and headed straight for the nearest sweetshop as the first unrationed sweets went on sale this month. Toffee apples were the biggest sellers, with sticks of nougat and liquorice strips rushing from the jars. One firm in Clapham Common gave 800 children 150lbs of lollipops during their midday break from school and a London factory opened its doors to hand out free sweets to all comers.

Adults joined in the sugar frenzy, with men in the City queuing up in their lunch breaks to buy boiled sweets and 2lb boxes of chocolates for their wives.

AROUND THE WORLD

"Ridding Australia of Rabbits"

For the third successive year there has been a favourable spread of the myxomatosis virus and the disease has combated the natural increase of rabbits. In many parts of Victoria and in large areas of New South Wales, South Australia and southern Queensland, a 90% reduction of the rabbit population had been reported. In one district, thousands of square miles of light sand country that had been kept bare by rabbits was now covered with new growths of grass and herbage ideal for stock feeding. Most of this county had been useless for sheep raising since the 1880s, when rabbits entered it from South Australia.

BURIED ALIVE!

The banks of the Jumna river

Swami Narayan Acharya, a Yogi went into a trance and had himself buried alive for nine days near Gandhi's Samadhi, on the banks of the Jumna in order to '*make contact with certain spirits to improve the world.*' However, he died either just before or soon after his pit was opened at the end of the nine days. The swami had developed the faculty of living without food or water during his pursuit of '*self-realisation*' and on previous occasions had been buried alive for periods of 24 hours.

Immediately before the swami went underground this time, he had spent four days without food and two months more sitting on a plank eating only eight bananas and six glasses of milk a day. The hole in which the yogi was buried was about 6ft deep, 6ft wide and 6ft broad and lined with wooden planks to prevent the sandy soil caving in. When the time came to open it, a large crowd gathered to watch one of his followers remove the sand, matting and planks which had covered it, and enter the pit to anoint the swami.

Soon afterwards the follower emerged and reported that it would be some time before the swami would be able to come out because of the difference in temperature inside and outside the hot pit. Later the follower reported that, after reciting briefly from the scriptures, the swami had told him that he no longer wished to remain in the world and then "*he drew a deep breath and the bird of life flew away from my master.*"

Six hours later, however, a police surgeon who examined the body reported that the swami had been dead between 12 and 24 hours. The Swami's body was then taken and immersed in the sacred waters of the Jumna. Narayan Acharya, who was 56, had adopted the life of a mystic about five years ago.

IN THE NEWS

Thursday 12   **"Blown Timber in Scotland"** It is estimated that it will take over two years to clear up the timber damaged in the widespread gales in the north of Scotland at the beginning of the month.

Friday 13   **"Royal Tours of Flooded Areas"** The Queen and the Duke of Edinburgh toured the Essex and Kent coast, visiting rest centres, factories and homes.

Saturday 14   **"Pit Pay Crisis Over"** The miner's pay dispute was settled with a 1s shift (6s a week) increase for 320,000 lower paid day-wage men.

Sunday 15   **"Coast Defences Hold"** East coast sea defences held as the new spring tides approached the peak. Better weather had enabled the thousands of men working on building the sandbagged walls to make better progress.

Monday 16   **"Bigger Grant Coming to Have Baby at Home"** An increase in maternity grant from £4 plus attendance allowance of £1 for four weeks is proposed for home births, to compensate for the £8 'saved' by mothers who have 10-14 days 'free keep' in hospital.

Tuesday 17   **"Order More Coke"** Because of the hard winter, Britain's homes have burned 1m tons extra coal compared with last year and the reserves are low. The coke allowance is to be increased by 20cwt.

Wednesday 18   **"2,000 Austen Men Called Out"** After months of negotiations and two strikes, an impasse has been reached because a former union senior shop steward, one of 700 men declared redundant last September, is among 270 who have not been re-engaged.

HERE IN BRITAIN

"Designing Perfect Shoes"

After scientific investigations, a new method of fitting is being used for children's shoes in some shops. A transparent shoe is used. The inside of the sole is marked, near the toe, with a green line, next to a red line.

When the shoe is tried on, the position of the child's toe in relation to the toe of the shoe can be seen through the transparent upper. If it enters the limit of the red mark, the shoe is too short. If the shoe is tried on a bare foot, pressure in the wrong places may be seen because it causes the skin to go pale.

AROUND THE WORLD

"Punch in Washington"

The British Ambassador opened an exhibition of contemporary original drawings from Punch in the library of Congress in Washington this week. The exhibition, which will last a month, has no objective other than to *'add to the gaiety of nations'*, although, as the Ambassador pointed out, *"If one people can laugh at the jokes of another there is very little need to bother about their other relations."* If the mirth shown so far by the American visitors to the exhibition, which concentrates for the most part of drawings showing British humour, is any guide, the Ambassador will enjoy a relatively quiet stay in the United States.

HMS HERMES LAUNCHED

Mrs Winston Churchill named the latest Royal Navy aircraft carrier 'Hermes', when she was launched in Barrow in Furness. It will be the first British carrier to embody three post-war developments: the angled deck, the steam catapult and the side lift. The launch was watched by hundreds of workmen who have helped to complete her and cheered by thousands of spectators crowding the shipyard.

The First Lord of the Admiralty said that the new 'Hermes', 18,300 tons and the last of four ships of her class, would be the most modern aircraft carrier in the world. Her flight deck is larger than a football field; her distilling plant is sufficient for most small towns; her generators could supply 10,000 homes without fear of power cuts; and two games of badminton could be played on the after lift. She is the tenth vessel of her name, the last having been a small aircraft carrier sunk by Japanese aircraft off Ceylon in 1942. The new 'Hermes' has a total length of 741 ft 6in and a beam of 90ft. Her speed will be about 30 knots, some five knots more than that of earlier light fleet carriers and she would take a wartime complement of about 1,400 men, most of them sleeping in bunks instead of hammocks.

The angled deck is a British development, which permits aircraft to land at an angle of about 8deg, so that should they overshoot the arrester wires they can fly straight off over the port side and the high-powered steam catapult, also British, is driven by steam from the main boilers and can, if necessary, launch heavy aircraft while the ship is lying at anchor. The side lift is an American invention to facilitate the movement of aircraft between the hangars and the flight deck during flying operations.

FEBRUARY 19TH – 25TH 1953

IN THE NEWS

Thursday 19 **"Breakfast to Go Up"** Controls are to come off eggs and sausages next month, and eggs are expected to go up 3s to 8s a dozen. Sausages will cost 4d or 5d a lb more, but they will contain slightly more meat at the new prices.

Friday 20 **"Call-Up Goes On"** National Service is to be extended for another five years when the present law ends in December. The period of service will remain at two years.

Saturday 21 **"Coal Prices Going Up 5s 6d a Ton"** The price of coal is to be raised by 10%. The higher price is necessary because of rising costs, including wages, and the large 1952 deficit expected by the National Coal Board.

Sunday 22 **"Disputed Island in Antarctic"** Argentina and Chile have been contesting British sovereignty in areas where Argentina has established seven military or scientific bases, and Chile three bases. Britain took action at Deception Island because the Argentinians were using British property and were becoming a "nuisance."

Monday 23 **"Union 'No' to Double Shifts"** Union leaders in Lancashire have flatly rejected terms proposed by cotton employers for working double shifts, the only way, they say, to combat foreign competition in the textile industry.

Tuesday 24 **"Deserters to Get Queen's Pardon"** An amnesty for 13,000 wartime deserters to mark the Coronation was announced by Mr Churchill.

Wednesday 25 **"Atom Drill for Our Troops"** The Commander-in-Chief of the British Army of the Rhine, said that technical advisers to give guidance on the use of atomic weapons, both for offence and for defence, were now attached to formations of his command.

HERE IN BRITAIN

"Question of Tradition"

The Minister of Food has been asked if ox-roasting will be allowed for the nation's Coronation celebrations. While meat is still rationed, this is difficult, but he is reluctant to stand in the way of traditional festivities. He has decided that any responsible body which has made a custom of ox-roasting at coronations, will be permitted to roast an ox during Coronation week provided the cooked meat is given away free to those at the festivity. He also promises that the meat ration will be satisfactory; eggs will have been decontrolled and tea will be freely available.

AROUND THE WORLD

"George Medal for GI"

The Queen has awarded a George Medal to Reice Leming, a 22-year-old American airman who saved 27 people in the floods in the Hunstanton area. The medal is in "recognition of his extreme gallantry on several occasions in rescuing persons who had been trapped in their houses". For four hours he had waded out to a line of flooded bungalows and back, dragging a rubber dinghy and bringing mostly women and children to safety. The Queen heard of his heroism when she visited the flood areas and Reice is the first foreigner to be awarded the GM in peace time.

CORONATION QUIRKS

With 'Coronation Fever' taking over, one newspaper wrote of some 'quirks' of a previous coronation, Queen Victoria's in 1838. The Queen gathered her strength for one of the longest coronations in history by eating two breakfasts before setting out on the state drive from Buckingham Palace to Westminster. Eleven thousand tickets had been issued for the Abbey and there was hardly room for the procession to move between the towering stands.

Fortunately, the ancient ritual of the Queen's Champion, riding through Westminster Hall in full armour, throwing down his gauntlet and challenging any person denying the sovereign's right to the throne, was omitted but a lack of planning meant those involved in the ceremony *"were always in doubt as to what came next, and you saw the want of rehearsal"*.

The Archbishop of Canterbury put the ring on a finger for which it was too small and the Queen wrote in her journal that she had *"to soak her finger afterwards in iced water to get the ring off, not without some pain"* and *"Poor old Lord Rolle, who is 82 and dreadfully infirm,"* she wrote, *"in attempting to ascend the steps fell and rolled quite down but was not the least hurt."* When the aged peer again came to do homage the Queen said, *"May I not get up and meet him?"* The altar in St Edward's chapel where the royal party could 'rest' when not needed, was covered in sandwiches and bottles of wine, and the Queen found the Crown so heavy that it 'hurt her a great deal' and she removed it for a time. There was some muddle about the Orb, because when the Primate came in to give it to her, she already had it but did not know what to do with it and when told she was to carry it, she replied *"Am I? It is very heavy."*

FEB 26TH - MARCH 4TH 1953

IN THE NEWS

Thursday 26   **"Ike Willing to Meet Stalin"** President Eisenhower has said he would go 'halfway – geographically – to meet Stalin if there were a chance that the meeting would do good.

Friday 27   **"Coping With the 'Cosh Boy'"** The Home Secretary said of the 'Prevention of Crime Bill', it would enable authorities to 'cope with the cosh boy *before* he uses his cosh'. The 'cosh boy' could then explain why he was carrying a bludgeon or knife.

Saturday 28   **"The Queen Visits the BBC"** With the Duke of Edinburgh, the Queen was entertained by a gala variety programme. Many popular radio variety artists were included and Mr Ted Ray was master of ceremonies.

Sun March 1   **"The Big March Fog"** Thick fog covered large areas of Britain, disrupting travel and hampering shipping movements in the Channel. The Queen Mary, bound from New York was anchored in thick fog off Cowes.

Monday 2   **"These 'Eggs' Are Killers"** Hundreds of 'ovoids' of deadly potassium cyanide were dumped on a rubbish tip in Greenwich. Children believing them to be pigeon eggs, took them home and several were badly burned when they put the 'eggs' in water to wash them.

Tuesday 3   **"Comet Crash"** Six passengers and all five members of the crew were killed when the Empress of Hawaii, the first Comet for use in Australia, crashed after taking off from Karachi airport on its way from London to Sydney.

Wednesday 4   **"Berliners Call for Refugee Airlift"** The Allies have been asked to start a new military airlift to prevent the steadily growing stream of East German refugees from swamping the city's Western Sectors.

HERE IN BRITAIN

"Steamer Rams the Nore Fort"

A Norwegian steamer ran into Great Nore Sands Fort, five miles off Sheerness, in thick fog. One of the seven towers collapsed and another rested on the deck of the ship, which went aground. The towers are not manned by soldiers in peacetime but by civilians acting as caretakers. Four of these men, who were believed to be on the sunken tower, were missing. The towers consist of 36ft square steel boxes mounted on 50ft concrete stilts, standing about 20ft above high water mark and joined by a catwalk. Erected during the war, they are fortified with several guns.

AROUND THE WORLD

"Automatic Gears on Jaguars for the US"

Jaguar saloon cars now being shipped to the US are fitted with automatic transmission. Most American cars are now offered with automatic transmission and thousands of Americans have driven only cars with two-pedal control. A drive in the latest Jaguar demonstrated the simple terms to which the automatic transmission reduces driving. For normal purposes the quadrant on the steering column is set in the 'drive' position, and the accelerator only is used to vary the speed from a standstill to the car's maximum, the change from the intermediate to the high gear ratio being made automatically.

IDEAL HOMES FOR 1953

Welcome to the Great Exhibition of this Great Year

The Ministry of Housing has taken care to see that in this year's Ideal Home Exhibition, where many fantastical types of homes are shown, there are also credible *'houses and flats built down to a price and furnished, if not on the cheap, at least economically.'* The Ministry's theme is how to get a decent standard of dwelling at a reasonable price.

A cottage flat, planned for a middle-aged couple with a 15-year-old son has the expenditure on furniture for a living room and two bedrooms kept to £500. The effect is not of luxury but of something that, say, a Civil servant, on the middle rungs, could afford. Although the materials are inexpensive, there is plenty of colour and there are money saving examples by giving items dual purpose, a bedspread and quilt combined and a small vanity table that serves as a writing desk.

A two-bedroom 'People's House', intended for a family of four, including two-year-old twins, is meant for those who fall in the £450-£500 a year income group, and the actual cost of the furniture and furnishings on display is £485, or nearly £550 if bought on hire-purchase. The items come from the cheaper range and the rooms are not big enough to call for large items of furniture, but even with all the designer's skill, families in that income group might not find it easy to furnish the house completely in one go.

For the 'Elizabethan House of 1953', a settee and two easy chairs would cost £5 10s 6d and the total cost of 'modestly' furnishing this style of home is £1,100, *'not counting the television'*. The lasting impression for visitors might well be that their ideal home will have to await the ideal income! But they can see that what is fairly cheap need not lack taste.

MARCH 5ᴛʜ - 11ᴛʜ 1953

IN THE NEWS

Thursday 5   **"Gravity of Stalin's Illness"** Moscow radio announced that Mr Stalin suffered a haemorrhage affecting vital parts of the brain, causing loss of consciousness and partial paralysis.

Friday 6   **"Stalin Dead"** The Communist Party bulletin said, *"The heart of the wise leader and teacher has stopped beating. His name is boundlessly dear to our Party, to the Soviet people and to workers of the whole world."*

Saturday 7   **"Malenkov Named as Soviet Premier"** Like Stalin, he is a Soviet Imperialist, the Cold War will continue.

Sunday 8   **"RAF to Have Fastest Fighter"** Vickers Armstrong are giving priority to the production of their Supermarine Swift jet, the plane which looks like a flying dart, has broken the sound barrier and will be the fastest in the world.

Monday 9   **"First Atomic Shell"** The Army announced that it will fire the world's first atomic shell 'using a projectile armed with an atomic warhead', from its new 280mm artillery gun in the spring Nevada tests.

Tuesday 10   **"Extra Pay for Army's Lonely Husbands"** A special, 'lonely soldier' allowance is to be paid to married men of all ranks in the Army who are serving overseas, separated from their wives. This is to counter the reluctance of men to sign up for long service.

Wednesday 11   **"US Fighter Shot Down"** Two Russian MiGs, coming from Czechoslovakia, shot down a US jet fighter in Europe, well inside the territory of the Federal Republic. The aircraft was, apparently, riddled with bullets and the pilot bailed out.

HERE IN BRITAIN

"Price on a Squirrel's Tail"

Efforts are to be redoubled to reduce the number of grey squirrels. The Forestry Commission is to introduce a payment of 1s for the tail of every grey squirrel killed and the scheme will be effective for two years. Sciurus carolinensis, a transatlantic species, was first released in Britain about 60 years ago and the 400 grey squirrels believed to have been released have now populated most of the woodlands in England and Wales with numbers estimated at 1.5 million. They cause hundreds of thousands of pounds' worth of damage by stripping bark from growing trees, mainly beech, larch, sycamore and oak, which then die.

AROUND THE WORLD

"Practice of the Tsars"

Mr Stalin's body lay in state in the Hall of Columns, the Russian trade union building, where thousands of mourners filed past in a slow, unending procession, said to be 10 miles long. The coffin was left open, as was the practice with the Tsars whose coffins were left open for the people to see that they had died peacefully and were not the victims of foul play. Pravda and all the newspapers throughout the length and breadth of Russia and the satellite countries appeared with heavy black borders and pictures of Mr Stalin. All theatres, cinemas and schools were closed till after the funeral.

EAST GERMANS SEEK REFUGE

REFUGEES POUR INTO Berlin
MANY IN PITIFUL CONDITION
The Mayor of Berlin, Herr Ernst Reuter, says that refugees are arriving "in an avalanche" and "no one knows how long it may roll." Nearly 1,000 a day fled to the West Sector last month. 20,000 wait to leave for the West Zone. "... the weary and ragged queue, which flow week through West Berlin . . . this island half-city like a fire-escarpment . . . Camp living, camps, is threatening the epidemic. Appeals are going out for shelter . . . "—*Berlin the News Chronicle Correspondent.*

SEND A DONATION— TO HELP ONE UPROOTED FAMILY
OXFORD COMMITTEE FOR
FAMINE RELIEF

DISCARDED CLOTHES Urgently Needed
Warm clothing is wanted quickly for the and children's warm clothing and footwear

The bombed sites round the central registration offices are packed with refugees as the exodus from the east continues, bringing thousands to seek asylum in west Berlin. These people have lost practically everything, the most they have managed to bring being a couple of suitcases or light hand luggage, but many smiled and seemed happy to have made it to freedom. They queue patiently outside the building, waiting to be registered and afterwards to be taken by bus to one of the 85 'camps' where they remain, sometimes for several weeks, before being flown to western Germany.

The 'camps' are mainly war damaged buildings and become packed with far too many refugees of all ages. Organised by the Red Cross and volunteers from within their own ranks, the crowded and insanitary nature of the properties inevitably leads to sickness. Each refugee has one hot meal a day and is given additional rations of bread, butter, sausage, jam and sugar and on arrival they receive two plates, three blankets, a chair and a broom. Children who had never seen an orange or a banana – unobtainable in the eastern sector – are given them when sick and nurses buy sweets for them with their own money. Even when the children are well, they cannot be sent to school and are looked after while their parents are away all day performing the tedious formalities required of them.

The tale of these people is always the same, they have fled either under the threat of arrest for some 'political' offence, a word which now covers practically everything which the east German authorities object to; because they were deprived of their means of livelihood for being kulaks or capitalists; or they had to work under such impossible conditions that they preferred to abandon everything they owned and seek asylum in the west.

MARCH 12TH - 18TH 1953

IN THE NEWS

Thursday 12   **"Third World War Not Inevitable"** Mr Eden said that in spite of the Korean deadlock, a Communist change of heart was not impossible, and the Soviet Union might see it did not pay to persist in a policy that united the whole free world against it.

Friday 13   **"British Bomber Shot Down"** An RAF Lincoln bomber on a routine training flight from Yorkshire was shot down by MiG fighters near the border of the British and Russian zones of Germany. Six of the crew were killed and one wounded.

Saturday 14   **"Protest at Murder of British Airmen"** The British High Commissioner in Germany sent the Russians a 'Note' on the shooting down of the British bomber protesting in the strongest terms against this 'deliberate and brutal act of aggression'.

Sunday 15   **"Prize Model Smashed at Tate"** A model of the prize-winning sculpture 'The Unknown Political Prisoner' was destroyed by a former Hungarian national who picked it up, crushed it in his hands and threw it to the floor saying, *"That's that."*

Monday 16   **"Marshal Tito Makes Historic Visit"** Marshal Josef Tito of Yugoslavia arrived in London, the first Communist head of state to visit the country.

Tuesday 17   **"Phoney 'L' Test Racket"** MPs made allegations that the driving test is a 'racket' in some cities, with a 'widespread feeling' that a learner was unlikely to pass unless he had taken lessons at a driving school.

Wednesday 18   **"Millions See A-Blast"** Fifty million Americans saw, on television, a blinding flash of red and orange which was the explosion of a 'device' on Yucca Flats, Nevada. It had the force of 15,000 tons of TNT.

HERE IN BRITAIN
"Atomic Attack Study"

The effects of an atomic bomb which was supposed to have burst 700ft above a football ground in Sheffield, at 11 o'clock in the morning were reproduced on a large-scale floor map at the Civil Defence Staff College near Bracknell. The object was to see if there was room in a typical town for the services needed to deal with the aftermath. Operations were planned by a civil defence controller; a police headquarters and a fire headquarters and great care was taken to simulate accurately the damage and casualties. It was estimated that the burst rendered 165,000 people homeless, killed 10,000 and seriously injured 9,000.

AROUND THE WORLD
"French Alcoholics' Bill"

A French wife may be ordered to separate from her husband if he is found to be a 'socially dangerous' alcoholic. A tribunal will then fix the allowance she is to receive from his income and social benefits and will be able to send drunks to special 're-education' centres. In the investigation of all crimes, misdemeanours and traffic accidents, the police are to arrange for an immediate medical examination to establish whether the act is attributable to the influence of drink. *"Consumption of alcohol is higher in France than in any other country, with grave effects in mortality and crime and in human misery."*

FEWER BRITISH IMMIGRANTS

M V Fairsea was chartered by the Australian Government to transport assisted immigrants from Britain.

The high rate of immigration since the end of the war has caused some of the Commonwealth countries to curtail the number they are now able to accept. The cost of enlarging public and utility services to meet the demands of their expanding populations, the ever-increasing cost of giving financial help to those who cannot pay for their own passages in full or at all, housing difficulties, and some setbacks in employment means the number of immigrants this year is likely to be well below the average of the last five years. The main countries of the Commonwealth receiving immigrants are Australia, Canada, South Africa, New Zealand and Southern Rhodesia. Of these, Australia has taken more from this country since the end of the war than the other four countries together. Between the post-war resumption of immigration and the end of 1952 Australia received 700,000 new settlers, bringing the population to more than 8,500,000. Of these, about half were British and more than 170,000 of them were given free or assisted passages.

The intention is to limit the flow this year to 80,000 to relieve the strain on housing, schools, hospitals and public services. In the first four years of the assisted passages scheme, 100,000 migrants from this country travelled to Australia on the nomination of friends and relatives who could house them; 43,000 were nominated by Australian employers with a guarantee of accommodation and 26,000 were tradesmen nominated by the Commonwealth Government, which undertook to provide living quarters in hostels. Of those who went out on a Government nomination, 10,000 were still living in hostels at the end of 1952 and the hostels scheme is to end. This does not mean there will be no assisted migration from Britain this year. The current Budget provides £4,730,000 for the financial assistance of British migrants.

MARCH 19TH - 25TH 1953

IN THE NEWS

Thursday 19 **"Parachute Trial at 29,000ft"** A parachutist was fired out of a Meteor III aircraft in an ejector seat at a height of about five and a half miles, the greatest altitude at which this feat has been attempted. The airman had only to jettison the hood of the aircraft and fire himself out, still sitting in his seat.

Friday 20 **"Earthquake Toll in Turkey"** An earthquake shook western Anatolia and killed 500 and injured several hundred. One tremor in Istanbul was the strongest in the city since 1906.

Saturday 21 **"Farmers to Get £15m More"** Subsidies are to rise, ½d a gallon more for milk, 3s a cwt more for fat cattle, 1d a lb more for fat sheep and lambs and 8d a score more for pigs.

Sunday 22 **"Seven Dead in Wreck"** Seven men lost their lives through exposure or drowning after the 18 members of the crew of the Grimsby trawler 'Leicester City' abandoned their ship, which ran aground on rocks in thick fog off Braebuster Hoy, Orkney.

Monday 23 **"General Neguib Says 'Evacuation or Death'"** The Egyptian Premier has demanded yet again that the British troops leave 'immediately, unconditionally and completely'.

Tuesday 24 **"Flood Coast Clear for Holidays"** BBC flood warnings which frighten people off booking holidays at east coast resorts are to be discontinued after protests that a wrong impression is being given.

Wednesday 25 **"Queen Mary Dies"** The Queen's grandmother, aged 85, died peacefully in her sleep. 120,000 people filed past her coffin as she lay in state for two days at Westminster Hall.

HERE IN BRITAIN

"Cats Are Out of the Bag"

To accompanying 'cat calls' from the back benches, the Assistant Post Master General was asked when the allowance for PO cats was last raised, how much it came to and did a North Ireland cat get as much as a London cat.

He referred to 'industrial chaos', *"Allowances vary in different places, possibly according to the efficiency of the animals. These servants of the State are frequently unreliable, capricious in their duty and liable to prolonged absenteeism."* There was no special rate for North Ireland because there were no PO cats there – presumably there are no mice in the buildings!

AROUND THE WORLD

"Russian Books at Fault"

Serious charges of sabotaging party decisions are made by Pravda against Russian State publishing houses, who are declared to have failed in their output to explain Marxist-Leninist ideas properly. Pravda calls for stricter control by the party over these 'inefficient' publishing firms and lists several ways in which the book producers 'have failed in their task.

They have issued 'unworthy books' and have not published suitable practical literature for students of political science. The attack comes closely on that made in Pravda against other Soviet newspapers which particularly criticised the papers intended for the younger generation such as the Molody Sotsialist.

NYLON ARMOUR VESTS

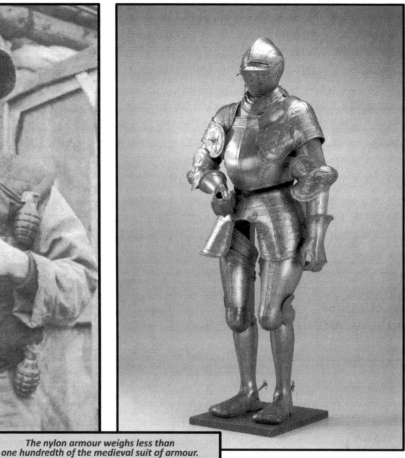

*The nylon armour weighs less than
one hundredth of the medieval suit of armour.*

A British version of the nylon armour vest worn by US soldiers in Korea is soon to be manufactured in Britain at a cost of about £20 each. The nylon vest weighs 7½lb and fits the body closely like a waistcoat or short jerkin, with a lightning fastener at the front and pockets on the outside. Its efficacy lies in its 12 layers of flexible, spot-laminated nylon duck (canvas). It is not designed to stop bullets but does provide protection against shell, mortar and grenade fragments, which cause most battle casualties in the Korean theatre at present. World armies previously favoured body armour of hide, scales, ring or chain mail or plate and its comparative rarity now, often attributed to the invention of gunpowder, is more likely because of modern mobile warfare. The soldiers of the latter part of the sixteenth century began increasingly to grumble about and later to throw away their 60lb weight of armour.

The modern British soldier is equally discriminating. As recently as 1942 the British Government placed a substantial order for three-piece suits of armour (breastplate, backplate and stomach guard) made of three 1mm light manganese steel plates weighing as little as 2¼lb in all. They proved less popular than expected and the order was cut drastically. Meanwhile, the US Army is testing 'lower torso armour' of the same nylon material. One type is a kind of trousers, the alternative resembles a sporran. When the modern steel helmet made its first appearance on the Western Front early in 1915 it was greeted with a degree of prejudice and ridicule but had fully established itself in the French, British, and German armies by the end of the Battle of the Somme. British factories produced about 7,250,000 by the end of 1918.

MARCH 26TH - APRIL 1ST 1953

IN THE NEWS

Thursday 26   **"Mr Churchill's Broadcast"** In a tribute to Queen Mary, he said, *"She was loved and revered far and wide, as perhaps nobody has been since Queen Victoria".*

Friday 27   **"Railways to Buy Blown Timber"** British Railways are to purchase soft wood valued at about £1,750,000 from the area of Scotland affected by the recent gales. It will be in the form of wagon timbers, sleepers and crossing timbers.

Saturday 28   **"Mau Mau Massacre"** One hundred and fifty Kikuyu men, women and children are known to have been killed by their Mau Mau fellow-tribesmen in a three-and-a-half-hour massacre at Uplands, near Nairobi, directed against all loyal Kikuyu in the district, mainly Government employees and 'home guards.'

Sunday 29   **"Queen Mary Lies in State"** The body of Queen Mary was borne in procession to Westminster Hall. Queen Mary's two sons, the Duke of Windsor and the Duke of Gloucester, with the Duke of Edinburgh and her grandson, the Duke of Kent, headed the royal mourners.

Monday 30   **"BBC to show 'Strangler of Notting Hill'"** Scotland Yard agreed the picture of John Christie, the main suspect in the Rillington Place murders could be shown on television. The bodies of four women, all strangled, were found hidden in the walls and under the floorboards.

Tuesday 31   **"Queen Mary Buried at Windsor"** About 4,000 people attended the service in St. Paul's Cathedral, followed by a simple, family, ceremony in St. George's Chapel.

Wed April 1   **"Christie Arrested for Murder of Wife"** The nationwide hunt for Christie ended and he was charged with the murder of his wife Ethel at Rillington Place.

HERE IN BRITAIN

"New Town's 2,000th House"

Mr Macmillan, Minister of Housing visited the nearly finished Adeyfield neighbourhood unit of Hemel Hempstead to 'open' the house. It marks something of a landmark in the history of the town and indicates a speeding-up in the rate of building, it is only 11 months since the 1,000th house was opened. Whilst there, the Minister also inspected a new type of house which has been built in 12 working days - an experiment to see how it compares with traditional types. The outside walls are brick, but the inner walls and partitions are of prefabricated gypsum plaster panels.

AROUND THE WORLD

"Children Learn to Goose-Step"

A series of German and Russian documentary films smuggled from east Germany and shown in West Berlin demonstrated Communist methods of indoctrinating children more vividly than reports or statistics. The film shows hundreds of boys and girls, goose-stepping to martial tunes, swearing Communist oaths with outstretched hands, kissing red banners and drilling with rifles. The spellbound look on their faces, the enthusiasm and exaltation is more disturbing than anything else which has come from behind the iron curtain and recalls the mass hysteria of the Hitler Youth.

QUEEN MARY DIES

The Coronation of King George V

Queen Mary's coffin

The simple setting of Queen Mary's funeral contrasted with the sombre magnificence that surrounded the last journey of her son just over a year ago. No drums and marching troops escorted her to the grave but there were hundreds of cards, wreaths and posies laid out on the lawns or leaning against the chapel walls. Splendid and sometimes beautiful as were the elaborate offerings from Governments, statesmen, and corporations, it was the little bunches of garden flowers from private people who had loved or been grateful to Queen Mary that were most touching.

Queen Mary was born Victoria Mary Augusta Louise Olga Pauline Claudine Agnes Mary in Kensington Palace in 1867 to Duke Francis and Duchess Mary of Teck. Young Mary, known as May, was the great-granddaughter of George III and a second cousin to Queen Victoria. At the behest of Queen Victoria, Mary was engaged to Queen Victoria's grandson Prince Albert Victor but he died shortly afterwards. Queen Victoria suggested that Mary marry Albert's brother George and although it was an arranged marriage, George and Mary fell deeply in love. When Queen Victoria died, Mary's father-in-law became King Edward VII and when he died, George became King George V and Mary was his Queen for 25 years. Her eldest son Edward became Edward VIII after the death of his father and on Edward's shocking abdication to marry Wallis Simpson, her second son, Albert, became King George VI.

The Dowager Queen Mary spent the remaining years of her life devoting herself to many charities, but she also liked collecting jewels and she was known for wearing several dazzling pieces of jewellery all at one time. She would wear several necklaces, brooches, stomachers, bracelets, rings and of course a crown, often mixing diamonds, pearls, emeralds, sapphires and rubies.

APRIL 2ND - 8TH 1953

IN THE NEWS

Thursday 2   **"Purses Delivered by the Queen"** The Queen distributed the Royal Maundy from St Paul's Cathedral. The ceremony is usually held in Westminster Abbey, but just now it is closed.

Friday 3   **"Now We See Hope of Peace"** MPs cheered Mr Churchill in the Commons when he said that the Chinese Premier's proposal on the exchange of prisoners seemed to offer a new hope for the end of the Korean war.

Saturday 4   **"Snow – Hail – and Sun"** The first day of the Easter Holidays yesterday started with a day of freak weather. One moment northern beaches were crowded with holiday makers, the next they were empty – with the crowds streaming into cafes and amusement arcades to shelter from the storms.

Sunday 5   **"Mr Eden's Tour Cancelled"** The Foreign Secretary is soon to have a gall bladder operation and has, therefore, cancelled his visits to Turkey, Greece and Italy.

Monday 6   **"Korean Repatriation Talks Begin"** Negotiations for an exchange of sick and wounded prisoners in Korea opened at Panmunjom. The UN has asked the Communist commanders to expedite proposals for settling the whole controversy over prisoners.

Tuesday 7   **"Washout Weekend"** One of the coldest and wettest Easters for years, greatly reduced the number of visitors to coastal resorts. The AA reported that outward road traffic was only half what it was on Easter Monday last year.

Wednesday 8   **"Naval Review at Spithead"** Detailed arrangements for the Coronation naval review to be held in June have been released. The Queen and the Duke of Edinburgh will review nine, seven-mile-lines of ships at Spithead.

HERE IN BRITAIN

"Headache Day for Pools"

The football pools' chiefs are worried about Cup Final Saturday on May 2nd. They are afraid that their coupons will be TOO EASY that day, and they are blaming the BBC because for the first time ever, the Cup Final at Wembley is to be televised from kick-off to finish. Most other Soccer matches have been brought forward as clubs considered their gates would be affected as many fans would prefer to look-in on Wembley rather than attend a local match. Only eleven English League games will be played – far less than the usual list of fifty-two games on the coupons.

AROUND THE WORLD

"Everest Climbers Short Of Oxygen"

The rear-guard of the British Mount Everest Expedition was slightly delayed in Katmandu for an examination of the oxygen being taken for the Everest climbers, Colonel Hunt having found some cylinders, taken by the main party, to be leaking. About 50 crates of supplies had to be checked, whilst an eager and persistent village audience watched. It included large numbers of ragged children, four Buddhist priests, resplendent in their saffron-coloured robes and a beggar girl impervious to invective. Happily only eight of 111 cylinders had inadequate pressure.

MAUNDY MONEY

1953 Maundy Service
The Queen being received by the Dean of St Paul's cathedral.,
Followed by the Duke of Edinburgh.

POLISHED SILVER MAUNDY MONEY

The distribution of Maundy Money, which takes place on the Thursday before Easter, is the modern development of an ancient ceremony said to be derived from when Christ washed his disciples' feet the evening before his crucifixion. In Britain the service goes back many centuries and Elizabeth I personally took part in 1572, in the hall at Greenwich. On that occasion a laundress, the sub-Almoner and the Lord High Almoner washed the feet of the poor people, and the feet then being, apparently, thoroughly clean, were again washed and kissed by the Queen herself. She then distributed broadcloth for the making of clothes and fish, bread and wine.

Royalty continued to take part but the last time the foot-washing ritual took place was in 1685. Several changes have taken place since then. Clothing was substituted for broadcloth for the women but that was stopped in 1724 and money was given in lieu. In 1837 William IV agreed to give the pensioners thirty shillings in lieu of all provisions.

For many years the ceremony took place in Whitehall Chapel moving later to Westminster Abbey. Today, the service is held in various cathedrals and the Queen, accompanied by the Duke of Edinburgh, has personally distributed her royal gift almost every year since her coronation. In addition to banknotes and cash (including a crown piece) which have now taken the place of all other forms of gift, the pensioners receive some of the world's most interesting coins presented in a small leather purse, with as many pence as the monarch has years of age. The recipients themselves number as many men and as many women as the monarch has years. In the days before base metal money, the amount was made up from silver pennies, twopences, threepences and fourpences and are still, today, struck in silver and polished like proof coins.

APRIL 9TH - 15TH 1953

IN THE NEWS

Thursday 9   **"Tube Trains Crash in Tunnel"** Nine people died and passengers were trapped in the wreckage on the Central Line between Stratford and Leyton when two crowded, homeward bound, commuter trains crashed.

Friday 10   **"Seven Britons Coming Home"** They have been held prisoner in North Korea since the summer of 1950 and were handed over to Russian officials to be taken to the British Embassy in Moscow.

Saturday 11   **"Southern Rhodesia's Vote for a Federation"** Over 80% of the electorate voted for a federation with Northern Rhodesia and Nyasaland. The Prime Minister has appealed to the opponents to rally now to build up a strong Central African State.

Sunday 12   **"London-Rome by Turbo Prop"** BEA is to become the first civil air service in the world to run 'turbo-prop' aircraft. The Vickers Viscount is to start a regular service between Britain and Istanbul, Cyprus, Zurich, Geneva, Rome, Copenhagen and Stockholm.

Monday 13   **"Russian Proposal for One Corridor to Berlin"** The Soviet's revolutionary proposals hold out little chance of four-power agreement. One corridor, 60 miles wide, between Berlin and Hanover, be substituted for the existing three 30-mile corridors (Berlin-Hanover, Berlin-Hamburg and Berlin-Frankfurt).

Tuesday 14   **"Not this Name"** The Queen objects to the naming of public houses after her children and magistrates withdrew their permission for 'The Old Stag' at Holmer Green near Amersham to be renamed, 'The Prince Charles'.

Wednesday 15   **"6d Off Income Tax: Purchase Tax Cuts"** In his Budget yesterday, the Chancellor of the Exchequer proposed taxation reliefs designed 'to improve our competitive efficiency, provide incentives for greater effort and to encourage private saving.'

HERE IN BRITAIN
"Married Women Resentful"

Dr Doris Odium, president of the Medical Women's Federation, in a BBC broadcast, said married women are going to hospital complaining of tiredness and depression. *"They are suffering from frustration and resentment; they feel they are 'put upon' and taken for granted by their husbands and children."* The biggest problem was that they do not receive any regular money for personal spending, *"If they want a pair of shoes or a coat, even underclothes, they have to ask their husbands for money. They feel this is humiliating and unjust."*

AROUND THE WORLD
"Seven Years' Hard Labour for Kenyatta"

Jomo Kenyatta, the leader of the Kenya African Union, was found guilty and has been sentenced to seven years hard labour for his part in the rebel Mau Mau movement which has terrorised and murdered countless Europeans and Africans for the past five years during its campaign for Kenyan independence. The aim being to rid Kenya of white and European settlers who had arrived since World War II and seized African land. The Judge said, *"You have persuaded them in secret to murder, burn and commit atrocities which will take many years to forget."*

BUILDING GUILDFORD CATHEDRAL

The building of Guildford Cathedral in only 28 years has been quick compared to the 480 years to build Winchester Cathedral! Built on the top of a hill this imposing building can be seen for miles around.

It is nearly 17 years since the foundation-stone of Guildford Cathedral was laid and during the years of war and austerity, the work which had begun before then, has stood forlornly on Stag Hill, dominating the busy by-pass and the houses spreading westwards from the town. Now there is a renewed effort to obtain money to continue the work and an exhibition of the cathedral, organised by the architect's wife is to open at Guildford House to show the work already carried out and visualise the finished building.

It will also show examples of the furnishings for the cathedral on which work continued even during the war. There is a banner, skilfully embroidered in silver and gold which was made during the war and contains the material of an evening dress! There is also a mitre embroidered with the design of the stag and a hill, an allusion to the site of the cathedral, a theme which recurs in many of the furnishings. The mitre was made in 1941, and is decorated with diamonds, seed pearls and fire opals. The walls of Guildford House are hung with examples of the work of the reviving Broderers' Guild. These amateur broderers are engaged on the blue and grey hassocks, of which 2,000 are needed and about 200 have been completed. The Goldsmiths' Company has presented the silver altar plate which is on display.

At one end of the room there are samples of the materials used in the building, a pile of bricks gives the impression that work is about to start but on closer inspection reveals that visitors, by paying 2s 6d (12p), may write their name on a brick in blue pencil and their names will be built into the cathedral. The aim of the organisers is to recruit 10,000 'cathedral builders', pledged to give a donation each year.

APRIL 16ᵀᴴ - 22ⁿᵈ 1953

IN THE NEWS

Thursday 16   **"Christie Now Accused of Murdering Four Women"** New charges made against John Christie mean he is now accused of four murders within 11 weeks, his wife and three other women.

Friday 17   **"Ike Challenges Malenkov"** President Eisenhower yesterday appealed to the new leaders of the Soviet Union to turn the tide of history and come to terms with the west. The conclusion of a Korean armistice, an Austrian peace treaty and the release of prisoners still held from the second world war, would be signs of Russian peaceful intentions.

Saturday 18   **"Extra Pay on Britannia"** Volunteers who have at least three years to serve will be selected for the Royal Yacht. Candidates will serve a year on probation and those finally accepted will get a special allowance of 1s a day.

Sunday 19   **"Sunshine for the First Day of Summer"** Although the easterly wind was cool, the sun shone throughout the country and traffic on main roads, on the first day of Summer Time, was by far the busiest since last August.

Monday 20   **"UN and Korea Begin Prisoner Exchange"** The Allies and Korea have exchanged sick and wounded prisoners of war with 100 UN prisoners freed under Operation 'Little Switch'.

Tuesday 21   **"Hope of Talks with Russia"** Commenting on President Eisenhower's declaration, Mr Churchill said there was need for patience rather than haste, but he hoped it might lead to conversations at the highest level.

Wednesday 22   **"Flying Saucer Aircraft"** *"So revolutionary that when it flies all other types of supersonic aircraft will become obsolescent"* is the claim made for the 'flying saucer' aircraft at the Avro Canada works at Malton, near Toronto.

HERE IN BRITAIN
"Queen Launches Royal Yacht"

Thousands of well-wishers greeted the Queen and the Duke of Edinburgh when they arrived at John Brown & Co., on the Clyde to launch the new royal yacht. In heavy rain, more than 30,000 people came to hear Her Majesty say, *"I name this ship Britannia."*

The rest of her speech was drowned out by deafening cheers from the 30,000-strong crowd, mostly employees of the shipbuilders and their families. The Royal Yacht has a displacement of 4,000 tons and has been designed so she can be converted to a hospital ship if necessary.

AROUND THE WORLD
"McCarthy's 'Young Bloodhounds'"

Senator McCarthy's young lieutenants Cohn and Schine have had a whirlwind European tour. They arrived for a brief stop in London, hot on the trail of Communists. They have been investigating American Information Service Libraries and their staff in Paris, Bonn, Frankfurt, Berlin, Vienna, Belgrade, Athens and Rome and wished to speak with the BBC in London. The object of US libraries abroad is to educate the readers in the American way of life, *"but,"* said Cohn, *"we have found many subversive books in them, written by Communists and reflecting the Communist line."*

LIFE ON A WEATHER SHIP

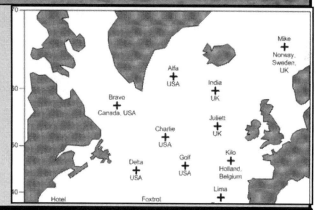

In 1949, 14 nations signed an original agreement to maintain ships on weather patrol and since then, British seamen and meteorologists have been on ocean weather ships in the north Atlantic where they carry out daily, in all weathers, meteorological observations at the surface and sampling of the upper atmosphere to a height of about 50,000ft. They send back reports by wireless telegraphy to the Central Forecasting Office at Dunstable.

Life for these men is an existence on the rolling wave. For a month at a time, they live in a converted corvette, 205ft long - which is a little short of the average length of an Atlantic wave. Weather ships when 'on station' are always drifting, as the depth of the ocean in mid-Atlantic is about 1,500 fathoms, which makes it impossible to obtain an anchorage. When off duty the men's favourite recreation is darts, once a week they have a film show in the ship's cinema and many of the crew have become expert bird watchers. On calm warm days, fishing, bathing and rowing races in rubber dinghies are popular pastimes.

One of the weather ships has a dog on board, which appears to be a keen meteorologist as it is always present to watch excitedly the release of the radiosonde balloon, which carried instruments to explore the atmosphere, four times in every 24 hours. Many of the crew are Scotsmen and on Burns night last year the haggis was piped-in, in mid-Atlantic and last Christmas the RAF dropped a Christmas tree for the men. Most of the crew are married and many of them live with their families at Greenock where the ships are based. After 27 days at sea the ships return to Greenock for 15 days and at the end of the voyage each man has six days' leave.

APRIL 23RD - 29TH 1953

IN THE NEWS

Thursday 23 "Shakespeare's Birthday Celebrations" Stratford-on-Avon celebrated the 389th anniversary of the birthday of her most famous son, William Shakespeare, with the unfurling of 82 nations' flags.

Friday 24 "US Order for 550 British Jet Fighters" An order for 450 Hawker Hunters and 100 Sea Hawks worth about £53.5m has been made under American offshore purchases for the North Atlantic Treaty Organisation.

Saturday 25 "Sir Winston Churchill" The Queen conferred a knighthood on the 78-year-old premier and invested him with the insignia of the Order of the Garter.

Sunday 26 "Parade of Scouts at Windsor" The Queen took the salute at the annual parade of about 1,000 Queen's Scouts in the quadrangle at Windsor Castle. Every county was represented in the procession and there were contingents from Scotland and the Republic of Ireland.

Monday 27 "Familiar Obstinacy in Korean Talks" Hope of an early armistice in Korea faded when negotiations, resumed after an interval of more than six months, halted at the fate of the 47,000 Chinese and North Koreans who object to being repatriated.

Tuesday 28 "Petrol Price Cut by ¾d" The Minister of Fuel and Power announced that petrol was now in ample supply and there was no longer any need to control their prices.

Wednesday 29 "Heroism in the Floods" The courage displayed by men and women during the East Coast floods was recognised by the Queen. Five awards of the Order of the British Empire, the posthumous award of the Albert Medal, three awards of the George Medal, and 20 awards of the British Empire Medal.

HERE IN BRITAIN

"Nest Eggs in Park Lane"

Deep in the middle of the Park Lane Coronation viewing stands, a mistle thrush has hatched out two of her three eggs. When the bird - the men call her Elizabeth - was first seen, a worried foreman consulted the Ministry of Works who ruled that Nature must take its course and the stands should be completed only when Elizabeth had brought up her family.

Instructions have been given that the top section of the staircase is not to be put in position until all the eggs are hatched. The mother bird is showing commendable patriotism in hurrying the process."

AROUND THE WORLD

"Mrs Eisenhower Ends the Feud"

The 176,000 'Daughters of the American Revolution' ended their 62nd Congress with a reception at the White House marking the end of a long and bitter feud between them and the Presidency which began when President Roosevelt, opening an earlier Congress, addressed them as 'my fellow immigrants.' This slight has now been forgotten and Mrs Eisenhower wiped out the insult by joining the select band and entertaining her new colleagues on the White House lawn. 'The Daughters', who were founded in 1880, are open only to direct female lineal descendants of a soldier who fought in the War of Independence.

Queen Victoria's head on her jubilee coinage of 1887 was changed in 1983 as it was thought unbecoming

King George V was struck in 1927 with the interlocking "Gs"

1937 three pence piece had colons instead of full stops

A mint set of 1953 coronation coins

The first of the new Elizabethan coins are now in circulation and up for public opinion. Traditionally, the minting of has been unpredictable with wild rumours abounding - many people still believe that 1864 pennies contain gold.

The yellow, 12-sided 3d piece struck in 1937 became the subject of many rumours: That it was to be withdrawn as a mistake had been made in the design, the colons after the abbreviations had been used in error instead of full stops and even that the coin had been struck without authority and therefore was not legal tender. There were so few in circulation that some people were convinced they had been withdrawn and paid up to 2s 6d for specimens. The reason for the scarcity was that millions were held by people as curiosities.

A new silver coinage for King George V was struck in 1927 included in its design the interlaced Gs of the royal cipher and the rumours suggested a mistake had been made and that the initials should read GR or GV or even KG. This interlacing of the Sovereign's initials however had been used on the coins of Charles II and William and Mary. The spray of six acorns on the new sixpence of 1927 aroused criticism, probably because of its unconventionality.

The design of the young Queen Victoria's head on her jubilee coinage of 1887 was so ludicrous that public opinion demanded its withdrawal. It was replaced in 1893. Her jubilee coinage included the four-shilling piece which proved a failure and was discontinued in 1890. Also in 1887, the Mint made the mistake of issuing a sixpence with a 'tail' identical with that of a half-sovereign. It was immediately gilded and passed as gold. The new design was dropped and that of 1837 which had just been discarded was hastily restored.

IN THE NEWS

Thursday 30   **"Scientists Describe 'Secret of Life'"** Two Cambridge University scientists, Watson & Crick have published their explanation of how living things reproduce themselves. They describe the structure of the chemical, deoxyribonucleic acid, or DNA.

Friday May 1   **"Berlin's Silent Marchers"** The vivid contrasts in the May Day celebrations showed the tragic position of the city. Within less than a mile of each other, thousands of people in the west formed a smiling, happy crowd for whom a demonstration is also a holiday, whilst in the eastern sector, a vast human herd was compelled to troop in silence past its Communist rulers.

Saturday 2   **"Britons Home from Korea"** Twenty-two sick and wounded British prisoners of war released in Korea, arrived at RAF Lyneham where relatives, friends, and tea, were waiting.

Sunday 3   **"Comet Disaster"** All forty-three passengers and crew lost their lives when a Comet jet airliner of British Overseas Airways Corporation crashed about six minutes after taking off from Dum Dum airfield, Calcutta, on the Singapore-London service.

Monday 4   **"Pilotless Jet at Woomera"** Watched by Ministers, an Australian-designed Jindivik Mark I pilotless jet aircraft and a rocket which could be adapted to carry an atomic bomb were tested at the Woomera long range weapons establishment in Australia.

Tuesday 5   **"Duke of Edinburgh Gets his Wings"** The Duke of Edinburgh has been awarded his pilot's "wings" during a private ceremony at Buckingham Palace.

Wednesday 6   **"Engineers Want a 40-Hour Week"** Delegates representing engineering workers believe that as production is up by 50% since 1946, their 44-hour week could be cut down and will make this demand to the employers.

HERE IN BRITAIN

"Mad Major's Swan Song"

In a single engine Auster, Christopher Draper, WWI flying ace, circled over Waterloo and then dived to make the final flight of his career ... Up the Thames and under 15 bridges to Kew.

His reason he said, *"I am flat broke. I have been on the dole for 14 months and I was determined that when I made my swan song flight, I would show everybody that at 61 I'm still capable of doing a job. I think I proved it – don't you?"*

Unfortunately, he had to miss three bridges, Hungerford Bridge, Kew and a railway bridge because of bad crosswinds.

AROUND THE WORLD

"Brave Gurkha Wins DSO"

The Distinguished Service Order was awarded to Major Purne Rai of the 10th Princess Mary's Own Gurkha Rifles, for gallantry in Malaya. The Major, who has 36 years' service took an under-strength and inexperienced company into the jungle and, by a series of brilliantly executed patrols and ambushes, killed five terrorists and located ammunition dumps, other supplies and documents. In another series of ambushes and patrols, he killed four more of the enemy. Eventually not a single terrorist remained in many square miles of jungle around.

THE QUEEN'S BEASTS

The ten statues created for the coronation.
Can you work out which is which by reading the description below?

Ten statues representing the genealogy of Queen Elizabeth II will stand in front of the temporary 'Coronation pavilion' outside Westminster Abbey for the Coronation in June. Called "The Queen's Beasts", there will be ten figures, each 6ft high, in the form of an heraldic beast supporting a shield bearing a badge or arms of a family associated with the Queen's ancestry.

Work is in progress in the crowded Hammersmith studio of their designer and sculptor, Mr. James Woodford. Eventually, all the small plasticine models will have been copied, life size, in clay, finished by Mr Woodford and made ready for the plaster casts to be made. The great Lion of England, wearing a crown which appears to have been pressed down firmly with both forepaws, will support the arms of the United Kingdom, and stand to the right of the line, guarding the royal entrance to the abbey; the Greyhound of the Tudors, with a crowned Tudor Rose on the shield; the Yale of the Beauforts – a mythical horned and tusked creature; the red Dragon of the Welsh Tudors; the white Horse of Hanover; the white Lion of Mortimer, this with the white rose of York on its shield; the Griffin of Edward III, supporting a shield adorned with the badge of the House of Windsor; the black Bull of Clarence whose shield carries the royal arms as used from Henry IV to Queen Elizabeth I; the Falcon of the Plantagenets, first used by Edward III.

The shields will be painted in full heraldic colour, but the animals will be left stone-colour, *"We don't want it to look too much like a fair-ground,"* said a spokesman from the Ministry of Works, but it would be tempting to see them in all the glory of silver, gold and primary tints.

MAY 7TH - MAY 13TH 1953

IN THE NEWS

Thursday 7 **"Railway Ship Sliced in Half"** The BR steamer, 'Duke of York', sailing from the Hook of Holland to Harwich with 437 passengers and 72 crew, was in collision with a US freighter. One section was towed back to Harwich and it is feared four people died.

Friday 8 **"Hope Grows For Truce in Korea"** Major concessions for the repatriation of prisoners were put forward by the Communists at the Panmunjom armistice negotiations.

Saturday 9 **"Our Jet Flies 12 Miles Up"** An English Electric Canberra bomber, powered by two Bristol Olympus turbo-jet engines, has climbed to a height of 63,668ft - over 12 miles - and in so doing has created a new world altitude record for aircraft.

Sunday 10 **"Uncompromising Speech"** Egyptian leader, General Naguib, says the evacuation of the British forces from the canal zone should not be conditional or postponed.

Monday 11 **"Secret Rehearsal"** Several hundred people, including some who had waited since midnight, gathered outside Buckingham Palace at 5 a.m. yesterday to watch the 'secret' rehearsal of the Coronation processions to Westminster Abbey.

Tuesday 12 **"Let's Talk Peace Says Sir Winston"** The Prime Minister said he believed a small, private conference at the highest level should take place soon between the leading Powers emphasising that outstanding differences need not be settled all at once.

Wednesday 13 **"Tornado Havoc in Texas"** More than 70 persons were killed and at least 400 injured in a tornado that struck Waco, a cotton town in Texas and San Angelo, some 200 miles to the west. The windstorms have left a trail of havoc over widely scattered areas during the past 10 days.

HERE IN BRITAIN

"Australian Oddity for the Zoo"

After 11 years, courtesy of Qantas Airlines, London zoo is to exhibit an Echidna, one of the most peculiar animals that come from Australasia. The native porcupine or spiny anteater is about the size of a rabbit and covered with a mixture of hair and thick, sharp spines. It is one of only two kinds of mammal that lay eggs, the other being the Platypus, but the Echidna lays only one egg and carries it about in a pouch in which the young lives after it is hatched. At about 4" long it is turned out, the spines presumably making it too uncomfortable.

AROUND THE WORLD

"Mexican Border Jumpers"

Mexican 'border jumpers' were coming into the US at a record rate of two a minute last month. In contrast, passengers holding American visas are often denied entry. Illegal crossings were made by 87,416 Mexicans in April, a figure that relates only to persons apprehended, and it is conceded that as many or more must have escaped detection. Given the difficulty of controlling a boundary of 1,600 miles with only 600 men, immigration Staff admit that there is nothing to prevent the *"whole of Mexico moving into the United States if it wants to."*

COMMONWEALTH TROOPS

Orders for the Coronation day processions to and from Westminster Abbey and an instruction for the accommodation, movement and administration of all British and oversea troops on Coronation duties have now been issued. The problem to be solved is to find or build temporary homes for more than 43,000 officers and men in London so that the armed forces of the British Commonwealth, from the Solomon Islands to Labrador and Southern Rhodesia, can be duly represented at their Sovereign's Coronation day. The processional challenge is to organise detachments from almost every unit in this country's fighting services and from the Dominions and colonies into their correct places in one or both of the royal processions on June 2.

The written orders cover nearly 200 printed foolscap pages and ensure, for example, that members of the Board of Admiralty will know where to meet their horses; that the Naafi has due notice to prepare 43,000 haversack rations (one cheese roll, one spam roll, one bar of chocolate, one portion fruit slab cake, one apple, 2oz barley sugar, with modifications where necessary for oversea detachments).

The thousands of servicemen taking part, and every band, groom, signaller, chaplain, medic, barge-master and water man, every eminent person riding or marching to their front and rear, now receive precise instructions for the great parade, for 'once the processions have left the forming-up place there will be no halt except in the case of an emergency.'

The prime concern is to prepare camps for 8,500 at Earls Court, 5,500 at Olympia, 16,000 in Kensington Gardens and 3,000 at Clapham deep shelter. 3,200 tents are needed for June 2nd. The administrative instructions include a wealth of minor detail and even warn the Coronation troops to bring coat hangers with them to camp (officers, 2; other ranks, 1).

MAY 14TH - 20TH 1953

IN THE NEWS

Thursday 14   **"Monopoly in Matches"** The monopoly is run by Bryant & Mays and the Monopolies Commission finds that the current arrangements governing the home production and imports of matches operate against the national interest.

Friday 15   **"Gen. Eisenhower and a Big Power Meeting"** The President said he had no objection to Sir Winston Churchill's suggestion for high level international talks but before committing the US, he would like some evidence of general good faith which, so far, has not.

Saturday 16   **"Briton Attacked by McCarthy Arrested"** The witch-hunting Senator McCarthy had the British editor of a left-wing New York magazine arrested and deported for refusing to say whether he is a communist.

Sunday 17   **"Egypt Says Suez Pact Will Soon Be Reached"** Agreement with Britain on the Canal Zone is not far off with the formation of an Anglo-Egyptian military commission for the phased withdrawal of British troops.

Monday 18   **"British Torpedo Boat Explodes"** It blew up with an explosion that rocked Aarhus, Denmark, and shattered thousands of windows in the port area. The boat caught fire immediately and was a total wreck in 20 minutes. There was no loss of life.

Tuesday 19   **"Plans for Double Assault on Everest"** Colonel John Hunt, the leader of the British Everest Expedition, has completed his detailed plans for a double assault on the peak, and has picked, but not named, his final team.

Wednesday 20 **"Students' Magazine Banned"** Cambridge undergraduates have been stopped from producing their magazine 'Granta' following its publication of a blasphemous poem. The editor may be temporarily expelled so that he cannot receive his degree until next year.

HERE IN BRITAIN

"Our Spending Habits"

There is an ongoing inquiry into the spending habits of 20,000 households in the UK to provide a revised index of retail prices. The last was in 1937-38, and there have been considerable changes since then because of the war and, especially, of rationing.

As well as spending on rent, rates, repairs, decorations and fuel, licences, insurance, education and season tickets, the questions include expenditure on food, tobacco, drink, household materials, books, newspapers, toilet articles, clothes, furniture, fares, holidays, and entertainment.

AROUND THE WORLD

"Fastest Woman in the World"

Miss Jacqueline Cochrane, foremost woman pilot of the United States, became the first woman in the world to fly faster than the speed of sound. The speed of sound is about 760 miles an hour at sea level and the Lieutenant-Colonel exceeded this in several dives. She also set an international air speed record for a 100-kilometre closed course of 652 miles an hour. The previous record with a jet aircraft on a 100-kilometre course was also set by a woman, 540 miles an hour by Mme. Jacqueline Auriol, daughter-in-law of the President of France and Miss Cochrane's rival.

HOMES FOR CAVE DWELLERS

The Prime Minister of Italy, Signor De Gasperi, has inaugurated, north of Matera (Lucania), a newly built village. This is to house some of the unfortunate peasants who at present live in the notorious 'Sassi,' or caves cut into the steep slopes of the deep ravine above and around which Matera is picturesquely, but unhealthily, situated. There are 3,000 of these primitive caves with walled-up fronts and lack of ventilation and sewage and it is estimated that to-day nearly 15,000 persons, or about half the population of Matera, live in them, a colony which has for long been a blot on the life of the country. Archaeological investigations have shown it to be one of the oldest continuously inhabited settlements in the world with evidence of human life from 7000 BC. Over the millennia, inhabitants had gradually dug deeper into the limestone's malleable rock to form homes, whilst some caves house underground churches with hand-sculpted arches, pillars and domes, complete with hand-painted frescoes.

The area's poverty and high death rate from diseases such as malaria, finally compelled the government to action, and the new village shows that Signor De Gasperi's, outgoing, Government, during its five-year term of office, has been successful in ameliorating some of these appalling conditions in southern Italy. The village, named La Martella, claims to be the beginning of the end of the Sassi caves. So far 50 houses, the design of which was chosen directly by the peasants from various plans submitted, have been built. Each house has three bedrooms, a kitchen-living room and a bathroom. Storerooms for farm produce, a stable for three head of livestock, a shed for a cart and about 850 sq yds of land for growing vegetables and fruit form part of each property, to which water and electric light are connected.

MAY 21ST - 27TH 1953

IN THE NEWS

Thursday 21   **"Welfare State in Peril"** Lord Beveridge warned the Government that Britain is moving away from real social security as he planned it in his 'Beveridge Report' and back to the sufferings and degradations of the Means Test days.

Friday 22   **"US, British and French Leaders to Meet"** A meeting between Sir Winston Churchill, President Eisenhower, and the French Prime Minister – but not the Soviet leader - will take place in Bermuda soon after June 15.

Saturday 23   **"1,400 Beacons for Coronation Night"** Beacons stretching from the Shetlands to Jersey, will be lit by boy scouts on Coronation night. Because timber for burning is so scarce, wood has already been collected and will be guarded by the boys day and night.

Sunday 24   **"Excellent Weather for Summit Attempt"** The British Mount Everest Expedition's push for the summit probably took place this weekend. So far as could be judged, the weather was excellent. It will be several days before definite news of the outcome is received.

Monday 25   **"Holiday Crowds in Storms"** The south of England had one of the hottest and sunniest Whitsun Bank holidays for years, 89deg at London Airport. But Scotland, north and west England, the Midlands and Wales had violent thunderstorms.

Tuesday 26   **"Johore Helicopter Airlift"** The largest helicopter operation since the beginning of the Malayan emergency was launched. In 24 hours more than 1,000 troops were carried into the jungle by the Royal Navy and RAF, a remarkable development in jungle warfare.

Wednesday 27   **"Lunch With the Queen"** Her 750 guests today will be her Ministers and representatives from 52 legislatures of the British Commonwealth, including six Prime Ministers.

HERE IN BRITAIN

"Coronation Crowns"

An Elizabeth II Coronation crown piece has been issued and is the first coin ever struck in this country to celebrate a Coronation. Coins issued in the Coronation years of previous reigns are often loosely termed 'Coronation' coins, but these are not special issues, they are the first of their particular series, struck in accordance with the Royal Proclamation authorising the general issue of coins for the new reign. The striking of commemorative coins and the issue of special sets of coins is a modern practice, the first being in 1887, the golden jubilee year of Queen Victoria.

AROUND THE WORLD

"Sicilian Bandits Sentenced"

After a trial lasting nearly four months, the central court of Palermo delivered its verdict, which took eight days to reach, in the case of the 45 men accused of serious crimes while members of the gang of Salvatore Giuliano, the bandit who, after terrorising Sicily for six years, was shot dead by the police in 1950. Thirty-one of the accused bandits were found guilty of complicity in 11 murders, 15 attempted murders and 14 kidnappings and received sentences of imprisonment totalling 600 years. Some of the guilty are still in hiding and were sentenced in their absence.

LEICESTER SQUARE

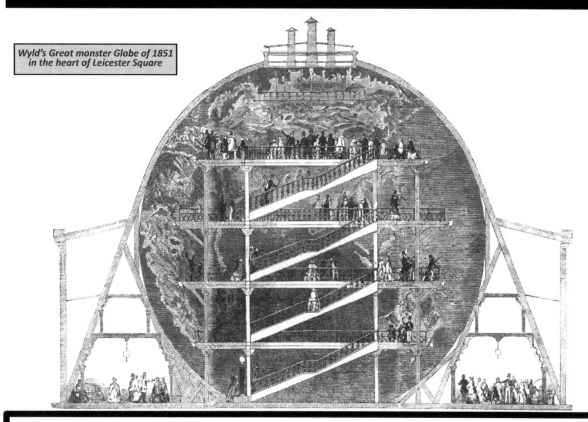

An exhibition of prints and records tracing the history of entertainment in Leicester Square has opened in the 'Lord Belgrave'. In Tudor times the common fields were used for grazing cattle and local fairs. About 1600, a bowling alley, pleasure garden and a tennis court where, later on, Charles II used to play, were built; later still, this was used for theatrical and boxing shows.

In 1851 an equestrian statue of George I was buried to make way for Wyld's Great (Monster) Globe. Wyld, a British cartographer and former MP, designed a hollow globe with the earth's geography represented on the interior surface rather than on the outside. A series of platforms connected by staircases on the inside allowed visitors to enter the gigantic relief map of mountains and rivers, built to scale, but vertically exaggerated to make them perceptible. This stayed for ten years, after which Leicester Square declined until householders purchased it for £13,000 and presented it to the public, opening in 1874.

In 1854 a large building of Moorish design had opened on the east side of the square as the Panopticon, housing a collection of scientific and engineering exhibits and possessing London's first mechanical lift. This building subsequently accommodated a circus and then, with the addition of a stage and other alterations, became the Alhambra Music Hall, which was gutted by fire in 1882, but rebuilt in an equally Moorish style to become a centre of ballet, variety and revue until 1936, when it was closed to make way for the present Odeon cinema. The Empire began as a panorama showplace called the Alcazar in 1880, soon became the Pandora Theatre and finally, in 1884, the Empire Theatre. It became a cinema but one theatre, Prince's Theatre in Coventry Street, renamed the Prince of Wales's Theatre in 1891, has survived.

MAY 28TH - JUNE 3RD 1953

IN THE NEWS

Thursday 28 — **"Four Men Shot as US Spies"** The execution of four men described as spies for the United States, dropped by parachute over the Ukraine in April, was reported in Moscow.

Friday 29 — **"Fishery Dispute With Iceland"** The ban on landing fish from Icelandic trawlers in Grimsby means Icelandic trawlers are not repaired in the town, their crews do not spend their money there and the manufacturers of stores and equipment are suffering too.

Saturday 30 — **"Restoration of Order in Kenya"** A new East Africa Command, directly responsible to the War Office, is to be headed up by Gen. Sir George Erskine to deal with Mau Mau terrorism in Kenya.

Sunday 31 — **"Tyres Fly Off the BRMs"** The ill-fated BRMs failed again in the French Grand Prix. Fangio, Wharton and Gonzales looked like finishing 1,2 and 3 as their BRMs were the fastest. Then Fangio retired, Wharton crashed and Gonzales only managed second.

Mon June 1 — **"The Big Wait"** Thousands of people spent the night on the Coronation route, having taken up their positions in readiness for the procession. They were not dismayed by showers of rain, and even sleet.

Tuesday 2 — **"Queen Elizabeth II is Crowned"** More than 8,000 guests witnessed the Coronation ceremony at St Paul's.

Wednesday 3 — **"Message to Everest"** The Queen sent the Everest Expedition a message. "*I send to Colonel Hunt and all members of the British expedition my warmest congratulations on their great achievement in reaching the summit of Mount Everest.*"

HERE IN BRITAIN
"How They Celebrated at Home"

Portsmouth: Warships in port were dressed overall and illuminated.
Birmingham: Many youngsters braved the weather in fancy dress parades.
Sheffield: Coronation concert by the Sheffield Philharmonic Orchestra and Chorus.
Edinburgh: A bonfire burst into flames on the rocky summit of Arthur's Seat and a fireworks display.
Bath: Processions, pageants and sports.
Northampton: A procession of decorated boats on the River Nene.
Beaumaris: Fireworks and torchlight parade inside the castle walls.
Manchester: A 21-gun salute was fired.

AROUND THE WORLD
"... and Abroad"

Singapore: Clashing of cymbals and gongs, Dragon and lion dancers.
New Zealand: A royal salute by an Army battery, the national anthem and a military procession two miles long.
Australia: Thousands of new florins bearing the Queen's head were circulated.
India: In Delhi, people partied on the hottest night of the year.
Pakistan: In Ramadan, when Muslims avoid gaiety, special Coronation films were on show in Karachi.
Hong Kong: Coloured portraits of the Queen, stilt walkers and colourful banners were on show in massive street parades.

GOD SAVE THE QUEEN

Queen Elizabeth II has been crowned, taken the Coronation Oath and is now bound to serve her people and to maintain the laws of God. After she was handed the four symbols of authority - the orb, the sceptre, the rod of mercy and the royal ring of sapphire and rubies - the Archbishop of Canterbury placed St Edward's Crown on the Princess's head to complete the ceremony.

A shout of "God Save the Queen" was heard and gun salutes were fired as crowds cheered.

An estimated three million people lined the streets of London to catch a glimpse of the new monarch as she made her way to and from Buckingham Palace in the golden state coach and the ceremony was watched by millions more around the world on television. The crowds, many already damp from their night sleeping out on the pavements to ensure a prime position, were drenched in the afternoon by intermittent showers but despite the overcast weather, the RAF marked the occasion with a fly past down the Mall and demonstrations of affection by cheering crowds of thousands continued outside Buckingham Palace until late.

During a hush from the throng, the Queen delivered her speech in the evening and at the end, a great cheer went up, followed by the singing of the National Anthem. The Palace balcony was flood lit and the Queen came out with the Duke of Edinburgh to wave for another two minutes before she gave the signal for the illuminations in London to be turned on.

Later, thousands more young people massed in the West End to end the day, singing and dancing together. The showers continued after dark, but they did nothing to dampen the enthusiasm of this cosmopolitan crowd, determined to celebrate their new Queen

JUNE 4TH - 10TH 1953

IN THE NEWS

Thursday 4   **"Developments at Gatwick"** Three main concerns have been addressed. 'Runways will be so placed, and the approach and departure of air traffic so arranged, as to cause little inconvenience to the main centres of population and industry. Aircraft will not pass over Crawley New Town and there will be very little night flying.

Friday 5   **"Nevada's Biggest Bomb"** The most powerful atomic bomb ever exploded in the US was dropped over the Nevada desert and its flash was seen more than 1,000 miles away in Canada and Mexico.

Saturday 6   **"Gordon Richards Wins the Derby"** The jockey, knighted by the Queen in her Coronation Honours list, beat Her Majesty's horse 'Aureole' at Epsom to win the race on 'Pinza'.

Sunday 7   **"Knighthood for Climbers"** The Queen has approved that a Knighthood for Colonel John Hunt and that Mr Edmund Hillary be appointed a Knight Commander of the Order of the British Empire. Sherpa Tensing is also to be honoured.

Monday 8   **"Korean Prisoner of War Issue"** An agreement has been signed over prisoners of war, but there is still no agreement on the demarcation line on which the armistice will be based.

Tuesday 9   **"Korea Bomb Shock"** Two bomb explosions by the communists rocked the war-torn South Korean capital of Seoul as the agreements were signed and the Korean war is *"as good as over."*

Wednesday 10   **"The Queen at St Paul's"** In bright sunshine the Queen drove in an open car to St. Paul's cathedral for a Coronation thanksgiving service. A fanfare of trumpets sounded as Her Majesty and members of the Royal Family were conducted to their places.

HERE IN BRITAIN

"Long Queues at the Abbey"

Thousands of Londoners together with visitors from overseas were waiting when Westminster Abbey was opened to the public for the first time after the Coronation. The visitors saw the Abbey in its full Coronation brilliance. Replicas of the regalia were set out in the annex on a table draped in gold damask and the Coronation chair with the Stone of Destiny beneath it had been turned to face the throne. When the doors were closed, the total number admitted in the day was 8,845. After July 4th, the special furnishings will be dismantled, and the chairs and stools offered for sale by the Ministry of Works.

AROUND THE WORLD

"Russian Controls in Austria"

The Russian authorities in Austria are to abolish their permanent control of passengers and goods traffic between the Russian and western zones 'in accordance with the wishes of the Austrian people.' *"Control of passengers will be carried out only if this seems necessary. Control of goods traffic will be carried out only if necessary, to prevent the bringing of weapons, ammunition and explosives into the Soviet zone and the taking away of dismantled factory equipment from the Soviet zone."* The western allies abolished such controls on the zonal border in 1947, but the Soviet authorities had until now refused to follow suit.

HEAD 'EM UP MOVE 'EM OUT

Cattle drives take cattle raised in the north of Australia across the interior desert to the markets in the populated areas of the south east over 1500 miles away.

This month, the greatest cattle trek in Australia's history was in full swing, covering the Northern Territory, Western Queensland and the Kimberley Ranges near the Western Australian border. It is estimated that more than 150,000 head are on the move and Britain should eventually benefit greatly by exports of prime beef. It is pointed out that the number is abnormally large owing to the extensive drought last year, which stopped all movement of cattle.

The cattle will cross the Northern Territory and end the long, arduous journey, across rocky ranges and sandy tracks at fattening grounds and killing stations in various states. Some will die on the way and all will lose weight. Kimberley cattle, bound for Queensland, will travel at least 1,500 miles and will have been on the road up to five months. Others taking the shorter routes will take three months on the trail.

About 100 experienced drovers, frequently aboriginal stock-men, are directing this record trek and the going in these vast open spaces requires men of mettle - tough, philosophical and full of rugged courage. As a diversion they sometimes fight among themselves and certainly pull no punches. At the end of the trek in 1951, fifteen drovers had a brawl at Newcastle Waters which lasted for more than an hour and a half. The drovers are in the saddle from dawn to dark and each must do his watch over the cattle. It can be intensely cold at night in the desert and most of the men grow beards and wear heavy coats. The drovers get good pay, and the job is well worth it. The rate is approximately 4s (20p)a head for every 100 miles of trek. The boss can make a very good profit on the 1,500-mile trip from the Kimberleys to Queensland, even after paying his men and providing food and horses.

JUNE 11ᴛʜ - 17ᴛʜ 1953

IN THE NEWS

Thursday 11 **"Unification or Death"** In Seoul, the South Koreans showed their resentment at the proposed truce terms with the north by demonstrations and stating determination to oppose any cease-fire while Chinese Communists remain on Korean soil.

Friday 12 **"Delta-Wing Jet Crash"** A prototype of the Gloster Javelin delta-wing jet, the RAF's new super-priority all-weather fighter, crashed at Bristol killing the test pilot.

Saturday 13 **"Liner Damaged off Dover"** The P&O liner 'Chusan' carrying 1,000 passengers and a crew of nearly 600, was in collision in sea mist in the Channel with the Liverpool cargo ship 'Prospector' about five miles off Dover.

Sunday 14 **"Le Mans"** The 24-hour Grand Prix d'Endurance, the sports car championship of the world, was won magnificently by a British Jaguar driven by Rolt and Hamilton at the record speed of 105.6 miles an hour.

Monday 15 **"East German Reforms"** The east German Government has taken the first steps to implement its recently announced programme of reforms. Measures include the release of some 4,000 political prisoners and orders for the restoration of ration cards to large numbers of the middle classes.

Tuesday 16 **"Feat by British Submarine"** A British submarine, for the first time, has made a 2,500-mile voyage across the Atlantic, from Bermuda, without surfacing. The vessel, the ' Andrew', an A class submarine completed the whole of her underwater trip using 'Snort' breathing apparatus.

Wednesday 17 **""East Berlin Russian 'Emergency'"** Demonstrating East Berlin workers clashed with Communist police and Russian troops and 16 died. The Russian authorities imposed a ban on all demonstrations.

HERE IN BRITAIN

"A Great Assembly of Ships"

The Queen, the Duke of Edinburgh and other members of the Royal Family, reviewed the Fleet at Spithead from the Royal Yacht Surprise. In brilliant sunshine the saluting guns of the Fleet thundered across the water and gun smoke blew towards the coast as the Surprise passed the old forts guarding the harbour entrance and steamed past the lines of anchored ships for more than an hour and a half. The Queen's Fleet was represented by more than 200 ships and three hundred aircraft of the Fleet Air Arm afterwards took part in a fly-past.

AROUND THE WORLD

"Russians Miss the Bus"

The Royal Navy wanted to host 30 Russian sailors from a Soviet cruiser arrived at Spithead for the Coronation naval review. A coach was sent to take Russian sailors on a sightseeing tour of Windsor and London and her captain was signalled, *"Facilities for 30 men."* The reply, *"Not 30, 150!"*
Frantic calls were made to order more buses but, in the event, the Russians didn't turn up, they were *"very tired after their voyage."* They also failed to turn up at a naval dance to which they had been invited in the evening.

The Queen's Coronation
BIRTHDAY PARADE
★ TROOPING THE COLOUR CEREMONY ★

The Queen, wearing a scarlet tunic crossed with the blue Garter riband and her black tricorn hat with the white Grenadier plume, sat slim and straight on her horse as Colonel-in-Chief of the five regiments of Foot Guards, and took the salute at the ceremony of Trooping the Colour on Horse Guards Parade. Trooping the Colour is a military parade that involves the seven army regiments that serve the queen grouped under the umbrella of 'The Household Division' and the ceremony is said to be based on an ancient Roman military practice in which the regimental standard was marched in front of soldiers who would then be able to identify it on the battlefield. Regimental flags of the British Army were historically described as 'Colours' because they displayed the uniform colours and insignia worn by the soldiers of different units.

A regiment's colours embody its spirit and service to the home it represents, as well as its fallen soldiers and before and after each battle, the colour party would 'troop' or march their colours through the ranks so that every soldier could see that the colours were intact. On the battlefield, the flags were used as rallying points and the loss of a colour, or the capture of an enemy colour, were respectively considered the greatest shame, or the greatest glory on a battlefield.

For more than 250 years, Trooping the Colour has commemorated the birthday of the sovereign as well as showcasing a display of army drills, music and horsemanship. Appropriately, this Coronation year, the Colour to be trooped was that of the 1st Battalion of the First or Grenadier Regiment of Foot Guards, of which her Majesty was Colonel for some years before her accession. The Queen personally presented the regiment with their new regimental Colour at Buckingham Palace about a month ago.

JUNE 18TH - 24TH 1953

IN THE NEWS

Thursday 18 "25,000 Prisoners Released by South Korea" In defiance of the UN, and on the orders of President Rhee, they escaped with the connivance of their South Korean guards.

Friday 19 "Egypt Now a Republic" Egypt's military council decreed an end of the monarchy and formed a republican regime with General Neguib as President and Premier.

Saturday 20 "Riots Spread in East Germany" The Russians have quelled the unrest in east Berlin but demonstrations and rioting have spread to many other towns in the Russian zone, and the state of emergency has been generally extended.

Sunday 21 "Big Three to Meet in Bermuda" It has been confirmed, the talks between Britain, the US and France will open on July 8th. The Prime Minister will travel in HMS Vanguard.

Monday 22 "Red Peppers for Heroes" The main party of the Everest expedition made a triumphant march through the last upland villages before the Katmandu valley. They were welcomed with garlands and strewn with a sort of red pepper as a mark of honour.

Tuesday 23 "Korea's 'Treacherous Violation'" The British Government have sent a Note to the Government of the Republic of Korea protesting against the recent release of prisoners. Sir Winston Churchill told the Commons that he is prepared to force the South Korean to keep faith with the agreement of 1950.

Wednesday 24 "Christie in Witness Box" Christie's trial for murdering his wife, to which he has pleaded Not Guilty, is continuing. He did confirm two statements in which he confessed to strangling three other women and in reply to his counsel he agreed that he might have been responsible for 'more killings.'

HERE IN BRITAIN

"Strike at the Court of King Arthur"

Two hundred knights and fair maids at the court of King Arthur went on strike. They were extras in the film 'Knights of the Round Table' which is being made at Boreham Wood studio and were to have appeared in the Guinevere-King Arthur wedding scene, but the wedding didn't take place. Guinevere, who is Ava Gardner sat in her dressing room all day in a cumbersome wedding gown, and two doors down Sir Lancelot – Robert Taylor – sat in his armour. The reason, other extras engaged through a theatrical agent were getting 3-4 guineas for a day's work instead of their 2-guinea union rate.

AROUND THE WORLD

"Spies Executed in US"

Julius and Ethel Rosenberg, convicted more than two years ago for conspiring to transmit atomic secrets to a foreign Power (Russia), were put to death in the electric chair in Sing Sing prison. Neither made any statement before dying. The Supreme Court had reversed the stay of execution granted to the Rosenbergs two days previously. It was the first time that spies had been sentenced to death in peacetime, although their actual crime was committed during war. There were demonstrations against the execution in London, Paris and Rome. Shots were fired in Paris and in Rome, police used fire hoses to quell protesters.

New! 3'

Spangles

Old English flavours

Spangles are double wrapped to keep all the flavour in and all the dirt out!

Since rationing ended in February, the quantity of sweets eaten in Britain has increased by at least a third. According to the National Union of Retail Confectioners, it is not just, as one would expect, the nation's children making up for all the lost years, but men are also taking to extra sweet eating. Shop keepers report that lorry drivers have the habit of buying bars of chocolate to eat during a long journey, many more office workers are sucking on boiled sweets at their desks and men have resumed the habit of taking home a fancy box of chocolates to their wives or mothers at the weekend.

The rest of the increase is undoubtedly due to children. During the years of sugar rationing, the custom of children having their own pocket money to go to the sweet shop lapsed and it was left to the possessor of the family ration books to 'bulk buy'. Now children are once again able to use their own pocket money to buy bull's eyes, humbugs, liquorice all sorts, toffees or chocolate, and although 6d (2p) buys only what 2d bought in 1939, the pleasure is just as great and already more sweets and chocolates are being eaten than before the war. The average consumption up till then was 7oz per person per week, when rationing ended it was 6oz, and now the average is 8oz a week.

The sweet manufacturers believe that when sugar rationing ends, perhaps in September, 'competition will become fierce' with many new, inventive lines, the packages and their contents will be even more persuasive than they are already and there is even a faint hope that the price of sugar will fall and the cost of having a sweet tooth will fall too.

JUNE 25TH - JULY 1ST 1953

IN THE NEWS

Thursday 25 **"All Night Queue at Lords"** The second Test match opens today, and people began gathering at the 5s (25p) gate yesterday evening. By 2am the queue, which included many women, had grown to about 100 and was getting longer.

Friday 26 **"Christie to Hang for Wife's Murder"** John Christie has been sentenced to hang for murdering his wife.

Saturday 27 **"Surplus Meat Off Ration"** The Minister of Food, announced that an extra twopenny-worth of meat a ration book will be issued to butchers, who will be permitted to sell off any not required to meet the 2s 4d (22p) ration for registered customers.

Sunday 28 **"Bermuda Conference Postponed"** Sir Winston Churchill has been advised by his doctor to 'rest'. The Prime Minister, now in his seventy-ninth year, is not physically ill, but is suffering from fatigue brought about by a long period of exceptionally heavy work.

Monday 29 **"Peer to Take Over Foreign Office"** Lord Salisbury is appointed Acting Foreign Secretary during Mr Eden's lengthy convalescence away from Parliament after his operation.

Tuesday 30 **"Train's Record Non-Stop Run"** The 'Elizabethan' express train from King's Cross to Edinburgh made its inaugural journey and managed the fastest time ever scheduled for the world's longest daily non-stop run. The train covered the 392 miles in 6hr 45min averaging 58 mph and reaching speeds of 90 mph in places.

Wed July 1 **"State of Emergency Ended in Berlin"** The Russian authorities ended the curfew in East Berlin which has been in force since the riots in June.

HERE IN BRITAIN

"The Art of Speaking"

"A young Londoner who cannot speak the local standard English, a hybrid between slovenly cockney and BBC 'correctness,' is likely to suffer a setback when he seeks employment outside the ranks of the manual workers." So says a pamphlet, 'The Art of Speaking', issued by London County Council. It concurs there has been some improvement and the more extreme forms of cockney are rarely heard from young adults and in schools, children are not often heard to drop an initial 'h.' Slovenly speech is, however, still common, typically the substitution of a glottal stop for the intervocalic 't' or 'tt,' as in 'wa'er' or 'bu'er'.

AROUND THE WORLD

"Exercise Over Europe"

About 1,800 aircraft of nine countries will practice war roles, in a fictitious setting which has an atomic-age flavour, during an Allied Air Forces exercise called Coronet. The regular air forces of Belgium, Canada, France, the Netherlands, the United Kingdom and the United States will be joined by contingents from Greece, Portugal and Italy. Coronet will cover the central sector of western Europe and its western sea approaches. A concurrent Army Group command post exercise is also involved, a fictional land battle will be superimposed on the air battle, and these will provide realistic targets and training in the operation of air support procedures.

SHERPA LIFE AT HOME

Following his successful part in the conquest of Mount Everest, it was announced this week that Sherpa Tenzing will be coming to Britain next month. For many years, the hardy men of the Sherpa race who come from north-eastern Nepal, have earned their living in part or in full by working as porters for foreign expeditions in the Himalayas. These climbers rely upon their Sherpas for carrying all their stores, erecting their tents, cooking and mending clothes and all for the equivalent of 3s 6d (17p) a day plus their food. Many of the Sherpas, including Tenzing, who work with European expeditions have settled in Darjeeling and have long adopted European ways. Tenzing is educated, wears European clothes and has top quality Swiss climbing clothes and reindeer fur boots.

However, most Sherpas live in villages on or above 10,000 ft and earn their living by trading with Tibet, travelling back and forth over the Nangpa La pass. They breed yaks, moving their homes up or down the mountains, according to the needs of grazing and crops. Most are devout Buddhists, and their typical garb is a shirt worn over breeches and high, embroidered Tibetan boots of wool and leather, with a thick brown wool coat, topped with a round Tibetan hat, the crown of which is made of a gold-coloured cloth with fur for the peak. The Sherpa women wear long skirts, often a drab colour, but over them they wear brightly coloured aprons, and their boots are decorated with colourful embroidery. Sometimes they wear the same Tibetan hats as their husbands, or sometimes a pretty little folded head square.

Despite some income as porters, Sherpas mainly lead a utilitarian life, practicing subsistence farming. Crops like wheat and potatoes are grown on terraces carved out of the steep, stony land. The yak is a vital animal, the milk being used for cheese and butter which is used for lamp oil and the dung as a fuel.

IN THE NEWS

Thursday 2   **"George Medal for Tenzing"** The Queen has approved the award to the Nepalese Sherpa in recognition of his achievement in the ascent of Mount Everest.

Friday 3   **"Palace Equerry's Surprise Job Abroad"** Group Capt. Townsend, an Equerry-in-Waiting to the Queen and recently, romantically linked with Princess Margaret, has returned to the Air Ministry and been posted as air attaché in Brussels.

Saturday 4   **"Everest Party Home"** The victorious Everest expedition party arrived in London to be greeted by a flood of congratulations. With them came Sherpa Tenzing, who shares with Edmund Hillary the fame of having reached the summit.

Sunday 5   **"Queen Reviews 63,000"** In Hyde Park, the Queen reviewed and took the salute of about 63,000 former sailors, soldiers and airmen and former members of the women's auxiliary and nursing services, summoned at her Majesty's own wish from all parts of the UK.

Monday 6   **"New London-Paris Air Speed Record"** Fleet Air Arm Lieutenant-Commander, Michael Lithgow, flew a Supermarine Swift fighter from London to Le Bourget in 19min 18sec, at 669 miles an hour and celebrated by breaking the sound barrier before 250,000 people.

Tuesday 7   **"Mau Mau Attack Royal Lodge"** A well-armed Mau Mau gang unsuccessfully attacked the Royal Lodge at Sagana, Kenya. The Royal Lodge, which was given to the Queen as a wedding present, is under constant police guard.

Wednesday 8   **"Korean Truce Talks Again"** Armistice negotiations at Panmunjom will be resumed after an interval of nine days with a meeting of liaison officers called at the Communist request. President Rhee's opposition to an armistice is as implacable as ever.

HERE IN BRITAIN

"Mutton? I Can't Give it Away"

A Hull butcher gave away his entire stock of ewe mutton, worth £6, as a protest again Food Ministry 'dictatorship'. *"Even then,"* he said, *"some customers said they would not have it at any price."* His action followed protests by butchers all over the country against a Ministry order that butchers who refuse ewe mutton should have their entire supply stopped. The Meat Traders' Associations decided on a policy of non-cooperation *"in that the trade will not be willing to assist the Ministry to foist unsatisfactory meat on the public."* Housewives would manage with less rather than purchase low-grade meat.

AROUND THE WORLD

"TV Wedding With a Pie Crust"

In New York, a young British couple, an actress and a writer, married on commercial TV watched by 3m American viewers. They stood before a TV stage set chapel, complete with altar and minister in attendance. The programme also showed viewers how to make biscuits from a pie crust mix, product of the chief sponsor! In payment for their appearance, the couple had an all-expenses paid trip across the Atlantic and gifts including a vacuum cleaner, refrigerator, suitcases, a typewriter, cooking range and a film of the wedding. Their honeymoon at a New York hotel is also paid by the sponsors.

WORKING PONIES

Ponies of all shapes and sizes between cart shafts had a day out at the annual Costers' and Street Traders' Pony Show organised by the Blue Cross and Our Dumb Friends' League in Kensington Palace Fields. Carts and ponies were gaily decorated with a Coronation theme that ran through all the decorations, with red, white and blue flowers, Union Jacks and portraits of the Queen and the Duke of Edinburgh. The first of these shows to be held by the league took place in Kensington Palace Fields in 1908 and for some years it has been held at Clapham Common but returned to its original home this year.

After the judges had completed their lengthy inspection the ponies lined up in the horse lines and delved into their nosebags. Near the end of the line stood little 'Mo,' the only donkey in the show, munching an apple and possibly thinking of the good old days when the show was first held and nearly all the carts were donkey hauled. Among the drivers was Mr. William Blewitt, aged 77, whose greengrocer's cart was hauled by the pony Polly, and who had been General Redvers Buller's servant and drove the General in the South African War.

The prizes were awarded and at the end of the parade there was loud applause for two horses which had been saved from slaughter by the Blue Cross, Dolly and Lucky. Dolly was bought by public subscription from the parcels department at Huddersfield railway station and now works for a Balham coal merchant, for whom he has twice won the Shire prize in the van horse parade at Regent's Park. Lucky was bought by the girls of Parkside Secondary School, Brixton, and now does light work on Wimbledon Common.

IN THE NEWS

Thursday 9   **"Cheaper Mutton and Pork"** The prices of imported and second-quality home-killed mutton will be reduced by 3d (1p) a lb and pork by 4d a lb. The cost will be met by an average increase of 14d (6p) a lb for first-quality home-killed and imported chilled beef.

Friday 10   **"Washington Talks"** With the Bermuda talks postponed because of Sir Winston's health, Lord Salisbury arrived in Washington for a conference of the three western Foreign Ministers, to review plans in the light of changes in Russian policy since Stalin's death.

Saturday 11   **"'Ike' Offers Food to East Germans"** President Eisenhower offered Dr Adenauer, the west German Chancellor, $15m worth of food to relieve the serious shortage in east Germany, and simultaneously appealed to the Soviet Government to cooperate in its distribution.

Sunday 12   **"Many Saved in Heavy Seas"** A number of people were rescued from vessels in distress off the coast of Scotland in heavy weather during the weekend. Heavy rain fell in many areas and there was widespread flooding in towns such as Bexhill and Warrington

Monday 13   **"No US Food Needed"** Russia refused the offer of food for east Germany, describing it as a propaganda manoeuvre and *'behaviour which would nowadays offend even the population of a colony, let alone the German people and its lawful democratic Government.'*

Tuesday 14   **"Large Coal to Be Imported"** To insure against the risk of a household coal shortage next winter, the National Coal Board is to import coal from western Europe.

Wednesday 15 **"Christie Hanged"** John Christie was found guilty of killing at least eight people - including his wife, Ethel - by strangling them in his flat at 10 Rillington Place.

HERE IN BRITAIN

"Baffle Wall Tests"

Tests are being carried out at London Airport of a sound baffle wall, shaped like a boomerang or flattened letter V, which has been built in an effort to reduce the noise and disturbance caused to people living near at hand by engine testing on the ground.

The wall, the first of its kind built in this country, is made of brick, 30ft high and 210ft long, with buttresses spaced along the length to give extra strength. The flat apex is 30ft long, with arms sloping from it on either side at an angle of about 35deg. Initial results were encouraging.

AROUND THE WORLD

"The Alpine Rally"

The international Alpine Rally is one of the most arduous motoring competitions in the world. The route of nearly 2,000 miles passes through France, Italy, Austria, Germany, Switzerland and back to France by way of Italy. Over 20 of the highest mountain passes must be tackled, demanding the highest driving skill and test of a car's endurance. Just as the Alps have always had a strong attraction for British mountaineers, so does the Alpine Rally attract British motorists. About a third of the 100-odd entries this year are British, and British cars will also be driven by some of the foreign competitors.

QUEEN'S BETTER BARGAINS

JUNGLE GREEN

Arthur Campbell

This month a lot was heard of 'the Queen's hard bargains' - national service men of bad character or poor physique whom the Services must accept as part of their annual quota. Much less is heard of 'Her Majesty's better bargains'.

The country has 313,000 national service men on full-time duty and 340,000 others in the reserve. This month a book called **Jungle Green** was published and gives an account of an infantry battalion in Malaya. The author, Major Arthur Campbell, recently commanded a company of The Suffolk Regiment during an outstandingly successful tour of duty and he describes the life which his men - most of them national service men - found themselves living, in the country where Communist guerrilla fighters have brought terror.

Since June 1948, some 20,000 British soldiers from sixteen regiments have been on front-line duty, searching out terrorists from the steaming Malayan jungle. Roughly half of these infantrymen have been national service men and of these, 67 have lost their lives and 115 have been wounded. For nearly all, the first entry into the deep forest is extremely frightening; insects crawling everywhere, ants and beetles of every size and shape and yet not one moving thing making the slightest sound. *"It was this eerie silence, which told on the men most."* The remarkable thing is that most master their fears and remember what their officers and NCOs have taught them in their few months of intensive training. Many young men are resilient, but it does not necessarily follow that these benefit as much from their periods in uniform as some older people take for granted. Is the national service man posted to Malaya luckier than his brother posted to Bicester?

JULY 16ᵀᴴ - 22ᴺᴰ 1953

IN THE NEWS

Thursday 16   **"The Queen at Fly Past"** Odiham yesterday saw the greatest display of air power ever mounted by the RAF in its 35 years' history. In the fly-past were 641 aircraft of 30 types. It was only the second royal review of the RAF, the first, commemorating the silver jubilee of King George V, in 1935.

Friday 17   **"Return from Africa"** Queen Elizabeth the Queen Mother and Princess Margaret had a great send-off as they drove through the streets of Salisbury on the way to the airport for their return to England after a busy two-week Royal Tour of Southern Rhodesia.

Saturday 18   **"Cause and Cure of Obesity"** 'Obesity is the commonest nutritional disease in present-day Britain', was stated at a British Medical Association conference.

Sunday 19   **"Step Nearer to Korean Truce"** The Communists agreed to begin preparations for the signature of a Korean armistice. If the South Koreans resume hostilities after signing, they will receive no UN support in the event of Communist counteraction.

Monday 20   **"Two Killed by Lightning"** A man, walking across Kensington Gardens and a youth, on a boat on the Norfolk Broads, were killed by lightning during the violent storms which struck southern England.

Tuesday 21   **"Brabazons to Be Scrapped"** The Brabazon I and also the uncompleted Brabazon II airliners are to be dismantled. No further expenditure can be justified as neither the civil air lines nor the fighting services can foresee any economic use for them.

Wednesday 22   **"Queen Takes the Salute Again"** This time at the Festival Hall Pier from some 150 craft as they passed up-stream during the Coronation year's, Royal River Pageant.

HERE IN BRITAIN

"The Big Bath Swindle"

Scotland Yard are investigating the plan to bring off the biggest betting coup ever known in Britain. A French horse running under the name of 'Francasal' won the 2pm race at Bath at 10-1. A few minutes before the "off" bookmakers all over England were flooded with heavy bets. When they tried to 'lay off' the bets on the course and shorten the price, it was found that the 'blower' telephone system exclusive to bookies was cut. The Yard is satisfied that 'Francasal' was switched for another French bay, 'Santa Amaro' and the £350,000 pay-out facing the bookies was stopped.

AROUND THE WORLD

"World's Most Expensive Grass"

New York's Central Park, home of the famous carousel, the boating lake, the zoo, the Tavern on the Green and skating rink, was 100 years old this month. The park, overlooked by some of New York's most fashionable hotels and homes, was created by a special Act in July 1853. At that time the surveyor who inspected the site reported *'a marsh, inhospitably studded with squatters, herds of swine, and stump-tailed cows.'* There were no special celebrations of the day, the park was filled as usual with youngsters playing baseball, mothers with prams and young lovers escaping the August heatwave by rowing on the lake.

THE ROYAL RIVER PAGEANT

On a dais, guarded by Queen's Watermen in their bright scarlet uniforms, her Majesty took the salute at Festival Hall Pier as some 150 craft passed up-stream in celebration of this Coronation year. It was the first large scale pageant to pass between Greenwich and Westminster since 1553, the boats manned by some 6,000 people, including the military bands. The Port of London Authority launch 'Nore', which has been used as the royal barge by the Queen during the Coronation celebrations, led, bearing trumpeters of the Royal Military School of Music playing stirring music and launches brought the Lord Mayor, dignitaries and members of Trinity House, with an escort of Doggett's Coat and Badge winners. The band of the Life Guards followed, and behind their launch came those of the Company of Watermen and Lightermen plus then, all the great Livery Companies, the three fighting services and civil defence.

Next passed twelve tableaux, representing incidents in the history of the river, from the Vikings up to the Victorian age. King John signed Magna Carta surrounded by threatening barons and the Black Prince was welcomed by the Lord Mayor at a London Bridge topped with a gory array of traitors' heads. There was 'Elizabeth I and the Discoverers' and the 'Bartholomew Fair' of 1668. This section was followed by craft of the Merchant Navy, Sea Scouts and Cadets and more tableaux representing the trade of the river in coal and oil, timber, tea and sugar. The finale was a procession of private craft, some of which had taken part in the evacuation from Dunkirk. Persistent rain didn't dampen spirits and the waterfront was crowded with spectators and as the last of the 'little ships' made their way past the Queen, a floating band of the Royal Air Force played 'Rule Britannia'.

IN THE NEWS

Thursday 23 **"Gatwick Most Suitable as Extra Airport"** Details of the Government's decision to develop Gatwick as the southern alternative to London Airport show that civil flying will stop at Northolt, Bovingdon and Stansted, and Croydon will be sold.

Friday 24 **"Cairo Parade of 'Commandos'"** The anniversary of General Neguib's revolution included a parade at which companies of 'commandos' - civilian volunteers who have done paramilitary training - marched carrying skull and crossbones flags.

Saturday 25 **"Food for 1m East Germans"** The Berlin Senate is to make food available to inhabitants of east Berlin and eastern Germany in spite of last-minute reservations by the allied authorities in view of possible Russian retaliation.

Sunday 26 **"Mr Eden Comes Home"** The Foreign Secretary flew home from Boston after six weeks in the US following his complicated gall bladder operation. He is to have a further period of convalescence before returning to full-time duty."

Monday 27 **"Armistice in Korea at Last"** It was signed in the great yellow 'Peace Pagoda' at Panmunjom, built of wood and straw mats and decorated with six-foot-high doves.

Tuesday 28 **"Footballers Have a Pay Rise"** The increase from £14 to £15 a week in the playing season and £10 to £12 in the summer, has alarmed some League clubs who could be obliged to offer players for transfer if they are too poor to meet the bills.

Wednesday 29 **"Repatriation of Prisoners"** It was announced from Panmunjom that the exchange of prisoners will start on August 5. The 12,000 UN prisoners include 7,000 South Koreans, 3,300 Americans, 922 British, 15 Australian, 14 Canadian and six South Africans.

HERE IN BRITAIN

"Yes, It WAS a Variety Show"

At the Leicester Palace, 'The Man They Cannot Hang' nearly hanged himself. Handcuffed and chained, hanging head down above the stage, he was cut down and collapsed after over six minutes! The knife thrower pinned his wife's skirt and panties to the board with a 12" knife.

The 'Wall of Death' rider drove off the wall and onto the stage dislocating his shoulder and finally, the fencer slipped on stage, his duelling partner cut a 12" gash in his back and the broken end of the blade whizzed into the orchestra slicing a violinist's bow in half! The show went on – with plasters and bandages!

AROUND THE WORLD

"Rush to West for Food"

East Germans, driven by hunger, defied the Soviets and queued in their thousands at the free food distribution centres of West Berlin, where much of the estimated total of 1 million food parcels are being provided by America.

Many people have been living for years on near starvation rations. Tea, cocoa and real coffee were unknown, while ersatz coffee was a luxury they drank only on Sunday. Skimmed milk was allowed for children, but adults had no milk at all, and many got the greatest pleasure from receiving a tin of fat, the Russian butter they had been provided from time to time, being rancid.

GREENLAND CAMPS RESTOCKED

Young Sound, Greenland, is only snow and ice free for a few months each summer. Resupply of the research community is done by ship and by flying boat.

For the third successive year the RAF is to make a series of flights within the Arctic Circle to assist the British North Greenland expedition, which is undertaking a geophysical, geological and glaciological survey of unexplored northern areas of the country. One of their main objects being to establish the depth of the ice cap which covers most of the country.

This year's flights are to be made in August by five Short Sunderland flying-boats and two Handley Page Hastings aircraft. They will carry stores out for the expedition and will bring home seven members of the expedition who have completed their one years' service. Other volunteers will go out.

The Sunderlands will leave on August 1st for Greenland where they will be based at Young Sound, on the north-east coast to await delivery of the stores carried by the expedition ship, the Norwegian vessel, 'Polarsirkel'. Three hundredweight of sugar, 100lb of milk powder and miscellaneous items such as torch batteries and bulbs, soda, washing powder, pressure lamps, pencils, ink and stationery and even an alarm clock, will be dropped. The Army will provide a beach party of one officer and 12 men to unload the ship, which will then return to Britain.

The flying-boats will then fly 70 tons of stores to the expedition's main camp at Britannia Lake, some 190 miles from Young Sound. If the weather is fine, this task should be completed in from seven to 10 days following which, the two Hastings transports will drop about 60 tons of supplies, consisting mainly of petrol for the 'weasels' - their tracked vehicles - to an existing *advanced* base known as 'Northice'. The stores which the Hastings aircraft are to drop will be used to enable the 'weasels' to attempt to reach the western edge of the ice cap.

July 30th - Aug 5th 1953

IN THE NEWS

Thursday 30   **"No TV of Party Conferences"** The Labour Party will not allow its annual conference to be televised this year. The BBC intended to televise this and the Conservative Party conferences, both of which are being held at Margate.

Friday 31   **"Home Leave for Prisoners"** The scheme, which allows five clear days at home, is to be extended. Its purpose, taken not earlier than four months and not later than two months before the earliest date of release, is to boost self-confidence, allow contact with prospective employers and to deal with domestic problems.

Saturday Aug 1   **"MiGs Destroy US Bomber"** Russian fighters destroyed a B50 bomber. Their ships picked up the survivors. The American Ambassador in Moscow protested to the Russians.

Sunday 2   **"Busiest Bank Holiday Since the War"** Blue skies and sunshine smiled on holiday makers leaving London and many other cities on the Bank Holiday weekend. Most resorts were full, and hundreds of visitors were camping out.

Monday 3   **"Food Rush Checked"** The distribution of the millionth food parcel coincided with the first official steps by the east German Government to stop it. The sale of railway tickets to Berlin has been forbidden, east Germans returning with parcels are liable to fines and Communist police are confiscating parcels.

Tuesday 4   **"Glider's Flight of 193 Miles"** On the final day of the National Gliding Championships, the International Gold Badge was awarded for a flight of over 300 kilometres.

Wednesday 5   **"Faster Flying by BEA"** British European Airways, is to introduce its nine Vickers Viscount air-screw-turbine airliners and 20 twin-engine Elizabethans, on new Continental and internal routes which will result in considerable reductions in journey times.

HERE IN BRITAIN

"Bank Holidays"

After a warm and mainly sunny August Bank Holiday most resorts had more visitors than on any Bank Holiday since the war and for this, we have to thank the politician and banker, Sir John Lubbock, who, in 1871 introduced the first law for bank holidays. Before 1871, we had only four holidays, Christmas Day, 1st May (May Day), 1st November (All Saint's Day) and Good Friday. In England, his Bill gave us Easter Monday, Whitsunday, 1st Monday in August and Boxing Day. In Scotland, New Year's Day, Good Friday, 1st Monday in May, 1st Monday in August and Christmas Day.

AROUND THE WORLD

"Christian Dior's 'Knee' Look"

The designer has raised a chorus of woes on both sides of the channel. In Paris, the biggest fashion controversy for years has blown up. In Britain they are calling it Dior's 'first mistake'. In the privacy of their own homes, ladies cautiously try out the effect of skirts finishing 17" from the ground and the owners of plump legs, skinny legs and long legs, all decided, *"It's too unkind."* Many dressmakers are saying their customers will refuse to wear it and Norman Hartnell, the Queen's dressmaker, *'just won't believe it'* until he sees it for himself. It seems to be 'Dior v The Rest'.

PROTECTED INNS

The Ye Olde Trip To Jerusalem in Nottingham, The Angel Posting House in Guildford and the Three Swans in Market Harborough all became protected inns in 1953.

During the past year, 500 English inns, representing many different architectural periods, have been scheduled for protection as buildings of outstanding historical or architectural interest. Not all them on the list are ancient, the fading splendours of the Victorian gin palace may have a chance of protection, if only to ensure that they do not become extinct. Many of the inns are close together as the surveyors move from one town to another.

Guildford's steep and cobbled High Street has five scheduled inns, including the 'Angel', a fine old coaching inn with a 600-year-old cellar and the 'Lion', where Pepys's writes that '*he cut for himself the best asparagus he had eaten in his life*'.

The 'Old Salutation' and the 'Trip to Jerusalem' at Nottingham are included and both claim to be among the oldest of English inns. Local tradition holds that the 'Trip to Jerusalem', built into the caverns hewed from the rock on which Nottingham Castle stands, received its name because it was used by soldiers going to the crusades. At Exeter the 'Ship' and the 'Turk's Head' are on the list. The Ship boasts a copy of a letter said to have been written in 1587 by Drake, in which he said, "*Next to mine own ship I do most dearly love that old Ship in Exon*," and continues with news of the sailing of the Armada. At the Turk's Head Charles Dickens is said to have started to write 'Pickwick Papers'.

Other inns mentioned include the 'Three Swans' at Market Harborough, which was well established in the sixteenth century and became the headquarters of both sides in the Civil War a century later and the Swan at Bedford, built in 1794 and containing a seventeenth-century staircase. The Brewers' Society intends eventually to mark the protected inns with a special plaque.

AUG 6TH - 12TH 1953

IN THE NEWS

Thursday 6   **"UN Prisoners Welcomed at 'Freedom Village'"** Four hundred soldiers and airmen who have been prisoners in Korea were given a great welcome in the 'freedom village' at Panmunjom. Among them were 26 British, all of whom were in good health and spirits.

Friday 7   **"French All Out Strike Threat"** A 24-hour strike in the French public services, including the railways and mines, has been called. The strike of post-office workers covers most of the country and there are threats in the nationalised gas and electricity industries.

Saturday 8   **"Pact on Korea"** Britain, America and fourteen other UN Powers warned that they would have to carry the war into China if the Communists break the truce.

Sunday 9   **"Soviet's Hydrogen Bomb"** Mr Malenkov's claim that Russia has the hydrogen bomb has prompted a drive for a new Anglo-American atomic partnership.

Monday 10   **"East German Ban on Rail Travel Again"** The week-old ban on railway travel to Berlin, relaxed a few days ago, has been reimposed. Nearly 100,000 parcels were distributed yesterday, bringing the total since the inauguration of the scheme to close on two million.

Tuesday 11   **"Whirlwind on Beach"** A whirlwind alarmed hundreds of people at Westcliff, Essex, yesterday. A slight breeze blowing off the cliffs suddenly became a gale which blew holiday makers off the esplanade and deck chairs and clothing were blown into the sea.

Wednesday 12   **"The Egg Shortage is Here"** If the demand for eggs does not abate the price will rise above the 7s 6d (37p) a dozen currently charged by retailers for Grade A products. Little improvement in supplies from home producers is expected in the next few weeks.

HERE IN BRITAIN

"The Channel Wins"

The Butlin race to swim the Channel promised prizes of £500. Seven competitors left the beaches at St. Margaret's Bay, Dover, and Gris Nez during the night. But all were forced to give up the attempt and no competitor completed the crossing.

Kathleen Mayoh, of Bolton, who crossed from France to England in 1952, entered the water at Dover to try for the distinction of becoming the first English woman to conquer the Channel in both directions. After swimming for 17 hours, she had to give up the attempt within hailing distance of the Calais beach.

AROUND THE WORLD

"French National Strike"

France endured two weeks of strikes in their public services this month, the railways were brought to a standstill with no drivers. However, the warnings were ignored by tourists and thousands queued at the Channel Ports.

Queues six deep and hundreds of yards long formed at Victoria station in London for the continental services. British Railways ran extra steamers from France to England to bring back returning British tourists who were able to get to the French ports and travel agencies in Britain devised ways in which holidaymakers bound for Italian and Swiss resorts were taken by special trains which avoided the French railway system.

A SEAWEED SYMPOSIUM

Pickled, spicy Seaweed.

The first 'International Seaweed Symposium' was held at Edinburgh and attended by investigators and delegates from every maritime country, China and Soviet Russia excepted. Most of us have a vague idea that iodine is or was extracted from seaweed. Some, if living in Wales or the West Country, might eat laver bread with bacon at breakfast, and nearly all at some time have, half seriously used seaweed as a barometer, or remarked upon its peculiar smell when washed ashore or stacked for fertiliser.

Yet to-day seaweeds are not only being converted into human and cattle foods, they are playing an enormous part in producing all manner of vital chemicals, in the making of plastics and as aids to surgery. They are in increasing demand for homeostatic powders, dusting powders, penicillin salts, a special wool invaluable for filling badly torn tooth sockets, surgical gauzes, a wax essential to successful operations on the skull, and a new first-aid dressing. Seaweeds now provide such diverse commodities as toothbrushes, chicken foods and fire-proof curtains. Madras is using them to increase its output of coconuts; the US is converting them into every conceivable commodity, from machine belts to tasty syrups, piping jelly and cosmetics; Amsterdam uses seaweed for the growing industry responsible for 'slimming – filler - products'

With increased demands for seaweed in all countries, improved methods of gathering are now the subject of continual research as the old haphazard gathering of cast weeds, torn from their footings by storm, is not enough to meet modem requirements and there are difficulties in supply. The Symposium reports that 10,000 tons of weed may be cast ashore at Orkney in a single day but the seaweed populations, though vast, are unstable and subject to fluctuation. This has been long recognised by the Channel Islands who have always controlled the annual cutting of the 'wrack'.

AUG 13ᵀᴴ - 19ᵀᴴ 1953

IN THE NEWS

Thursday 13   **"Scorcher: Temperatures in the 90s"** The scorching heat set off many heath fires and thunderstorms in the south and west caused floods and damage.

Friday 14   **"Greek Island Earthquakes"** Helicopters surveying the destruction in Cephalonia found that all the towns lay in ruins. Many hundreds of people are thought to have been killed.

Saturday 15   **"£6m Colliery for Wales"** A broad valley, roughly five miles square, between Amman Valley and Swansea Valley is to become the site of a second modern horizon-mining development. With reserves of 134 million tons, the work will employ 2,000 men.

Sunday 16   **"Shah Flees With His Queen"** Dr Moussadek, the Persian Prime Minister, has crushed an attempted coup by officers of the Shah's Imperial Guards. The Shah and Queen Soraya fled to Baghdad before going on to Europe.

Monday 17   **"Viaduct Train Crash"** Two trains collided on the Irk Valley viaduct near Manchester in the early hours of yesterday. One coach plunged 90ft to the river bed below.Ten people died and fifty nine were taken to hospital.

Tuesday 18   **"Death Penalty for Looters"** The situation in the stricken Ionian Islands was reported to be improving steadily but the military governor issued orders that looters should be shot on the spot. Thirty-five alleged looters have already been arrested.

Wednesday 19   **"Ex-Prisoners on Way Home"** The troopship 'Asturias' has left for Southampton carrying one officer and 340 other ranks recently released from the Communist camps in North Korea. The repatriates were in high spirits and good health and the ship is expected to reach Britain about September 17.

HERE IN BRITAIN
"Cricket Fever"

Britain went cricket mad on Tuesday this week as England smashed back at the Australians in the last, deciding, Test for the Ashes. Ten British passengers were still sitting in their BEA plane fifteen minutes after it had landed at Brussels – not until the radio operator had picked up the latest score would they leave the plane. All over the world radio operators in British airliners were tuning into BBC broadcasts of the game and the BBC cancelled all advertised programmes on the Light Programme to allow the cricket commentary to continue uninterrupted until close of play at 6.30pm. The Ashes are in sight!

AROUND THE WORLD
"Greek Islands Devastated"

The Ionian Islands suffered a terrible series of earthquakes that began on the 8 August. There were over 113 recorded earthquakes in the region between Cefalonia and Zakynthos, but the most destructive was the earthquake of August 12ᵗʰ which measured 7.2 on the Richter scale and caused widespread devastation and deaths. Cephalonia was thrust upwards by about 60cm within a few seconds, by a force equivalent to 63million tons of explosive. The island lies just east of a major tectonic fault where the European and the Aegean plates meet. A worldwide relief effort was mounted with ships of the Royal Navy being first on the scene.

PEARL FISHING

A special Australian emissary has gone to Athens to look at the possibility of using sponge fishermen of the island of Kalymnos in the Aegean Sea as pearl divers in the Broome area, on Australia's north-west flank. The 15,000 inhabitants of Kalymnos, a small, barren rock island, made their livelihood in the past almost exclusively from sponge fishing, but during the last two years the trade has died, and the island is abandoned.

On the other hand, Australia, has the world's largest and finest pearl shell beds on its northern borders, and before the war had a pearling fleet of about 300 luggers manned mostly by Asians. Rather than readmit Japanese divers, they are looking for pearl divers among the Greeks.

Two factors will determine the practicability of the scheme, whether the Kalymnos fishermen are prepared to emigrate to Australia, and, whether they have or could acquire the aptitude for pearl diving. It is expected that a few will visit Australia so that they can see for themselves the kind of life they would be expected to lead and the greater rigour of pearl diving. The Japanese pearl divers are able to descend to as much as 20 fathoms below the sea level, more than the Malays who can descend to only 12 to 14 fathoms.

The Greeks will therefore have to face quite a strenuous test, but if the experience of the Dodecanese fishermen who emigrated to the southern coast of Florida can be taken as an indication, the men from Kalymnos should stand a fair chance. For Australia, pearl shell has become a good source of revenue and last year reached the unprecedented price of $A700 per ton. The occasional prize pearl, such as 'Star of the West', valued at $A14,000, is, of course, an additional incentive.

AUG 20ᵀᴴ - 26ᵀᴴ 1953

IN THE NEWS

Thursday 20 **"England Regain the Ashes"** After 20 years in the series against Australia, and 27 years on British soil, England at last won back the Ashes in this Coronation year with a victory by eight wickets in the final Test match.

Friday 21 **"Russia Explodes Hydrogen Bomb"** The announcement, in Pravda, stated that the explosion was 'of great strength' and 'showed that the power of the hydrogen bomb is many times greater than the power of atomic bombs.'

Saturday 22 **"Dr Moussadek Arrested"** The supporters of the Shah have ousted the Persian Prime Minister. General Zahedi has assumed control in the capital.

Sunday 23 **"Mau Mau Gangs Offer"** The Governor of Kenya announced plans for a surrender offer to the terrorists following receipt of Notes from Mau Mau leaders offering to disband their gangs and end their activities if suitable terms are forthcoming.

Monday 24 **"Coach Crashed Down Ravine"** Six people, including the driver, were killed and 22 injured when the coach in which they were travelling from Penrith to Morecambe crashed through a wall while descending Shap Fell. As it somersaulted down the slope, flinging people and their seats out in all directions, the coach gradually disintegrated.

Tuesday 25 **"Buried Alive for 12 Days"** Two women were rescued alive beneath the ruins of their home, destroyed in an earthquake on Cephalonia.

Wednesday 26 **"Electrician's 'Guerilla' Pay War"** More than 1,000 electricians at 10 sites in various parts of the country went on strike. Among the sites affected were two atomic research establishments, oil refineries, motor works, steel works and London Airport.

HERE IN BRITAIN

"Roman Villa in the Back Garden"

Three months ago, the tenant of a new council house at Downton in Wiltshire tried to sink a washing post into his back garden but he found it could not go down further than 14 inches. He did a little investigating and found the obstruction to be a tessellated Roman floor, presumably of a villa.

Now a team of unpaid archaeologists, working mostly in evenings and at weekends, are digging trial trenches in an area, 25 or 30 yards square, which coincides with the back gardens of Nos 12 and 13, Moot Close. The first phase of an estate of 160 pre-fabricated concrete houses.

AROUND THE WORLD

"Worthless British Birth Certificate"

Argentina's 120-year-old claim to sovereignty over the Falkland Isles was again asserted this week when an Argentine federal Judge ordered that Rodolfo Carlos Linde de Aranpreis, a British subject born in the Falklands in January, 1910, be registered as an Argentine citizen. The Judge said that his birth certificate, issued by British authorities in the Falklands was worthless because Argentina had inherited the Falklands from Spain, whose rights dated from the discovery of America. The Judge ruled that he might continue to call himself Rudolph Smith as this was the name by which he was known, and which appeared in his documents.

BARTLEMAS DAY

St Bart's Hospital in London (left) and St Bartholomew's Hospital in Sandwich (below) which is the centre of giving Bart's Buns to children on Bartlemas Day.

Saint Bartholomew was supposedly martyred by being flayed alive and this connection has made him the patron saint to butchers and tanners and by extension to bookbinders, for one of their traditional materials for binding books is leather. The Saint is best associated with two institutions, St Bart's Hospital in London and the ancient St Bartholomew's Fair. However, the Cinque Port of Sandwich in Kent also celebrates St Bartholomew's Day each August 24th. Among the most cherished institutions of the town is their St. Bartholomew's Hospital, not a traditional place for the sick, but a tranquil setting for the aged men and women of the town.

The records of the hospital give full details of its foundation in the reign of Richard the Lionheart, who landed at Sandwich on his return from the Crusades. There were four founding knights, and one of them, Sir Henry de Sandwich, has his tomb in the chapel of the hospital. These knights gave their land to provide a home for maimed mariners and the poor and elderly of the city to end their days in peace, and for more than 750 years, the 'brothers and sisters,' chosen by town worthies have lived on this same quiet site.

About 50 years ago the old hospital building of the middle ages was replaced by a quadrangle of little cottages, each standing in its garden with the ancient chapel, with its Norman arches, remaining in the centre. A service is held in the chapel on Bartlemas Day following which, the children of Sandwich run round the chapel and receive a current bun from the trustees of the hospital. The adults who attend the service are presented with a less edible 'St Bart's biscuit', a wafer stamped with the arms of Sandwich and the legend of the foundation.

AUG 27TH - SEPT 2ND 1953

IN THE NEWS

Thursday 27   **"Bottom of the Sea"** Auguste Piccard, the first man to reach the stratosphere in a balloon, has now touched the bottom of the sea, 3,451 ft down, in his ten-ton submarine like bathyscaphe off the Isle of Capri.

Friday 28   **"New Troops for Kenya"** Britain is backing her surrender demand to the Mau Mau by flying out more troops, trained and equipped for guerrilla fighting in Kenya's forests.

Saturday 29   **"Mock Attacks on Liners"** Transatlantic liners, including the Queen Elizabeth and the Queen Mary are to take part in Exercise Mariner. They will represent fast, independently routed troop ships and be under attack by submarines, aircraft, and surface raiders.

Sunday 30   **"More Than 10,600 UN Prisoners Returned"** Only 2,000 now remain. Today a further 25 Britons, including eight officers and 12 sergeants came back, confirming the belief that the Communists held back these ranks until last.

Monday 31   **"Disastrous Storm in Cephalonia"** A violent rainstorm struck the earthquake-stricken island of Cephalonia spreading havoc in the temporary camps of the survivors.

Tuesday Sept 1   **"New Bread"** Whiter bread has appeared in the shops for the first time since 1939, but it looked so much like the ordinary 'National' bread that bakers had to label it "White Loaf". The 14oz loaf was sold for 5¾d (2p) in Inner London and 6d outside.

Wednesday 2   **"Electricians Strike Spreading"** More than 2,000 members of the ETU are idle. Strike action has been taken at two oil refineries, two atomic plants, motor and steel works, the radio and engineering exhibitions and the new White City television studios.

HERE IN BRITAIN

"Losing Noughts and Crosses"

Among the many electronic devices on show at the National Radio Show at Earls Court, visitors to the exhibition will see a machine which can pit its electronic brain against the human mind in a game of noughts and crosses, and the annoying thing about it, is that it always wins.

It will not play according to fixed rules (this does not mean that it cheats) but varies its attack. If, for instance, it has the first move, it may play into any of the nine squares and even if the human opponent makes the first move, it is still impossible to beat.

AROUND THE WORLD

"The Big Apple Cooks"

At 1 o'clock on September 1st, the temperature rose above 91deg, and it became the eighth successive day in New York of heat exceeding 90deg. It followed five successive days of more than 95deg. – two of them at 97deg. No spell of such intense heat has ever lasted this long since the New York weather bureau began keeping records 82 years ago.

The heat spell is over all the eastern United States and the Middle West, held there by a stagnant high-pressure system. Crops have been ruined by heat and drought, and many fires have broken out in the parched woods.

LIGHTING UP THE SEASIDE

DECORATIVE CANOPY

FLORAL ARCH CENOTAPH

THE SWAN LAKE TABLEAU

BLACKPOOL
ILLUMINATIONS

THE LIFEBOAT TRAM

THE GONDOLA TRAM

The big seaside resorts' publicity departments do not exaggerate when they say that this year's illuminations are bigger, brighter and better than before. The public response is the important thing, and the attraction of the lights help to prolong the holiday season until the end of September and even into October. Blackpool claims that it led the way in large- scale schemes of illumination in 1912 and this year it is the town's twenty-first annual display. Southport says there have been illuminations in the town for 40 years, and Morecambe maintains it was the first resort to use candles to light up foliage along the promenade. George Formby will switch on the Blackpool illuminations this year, and the staff of 150 are working to get the display completed. Most of the tableaux are designed by artists and they are built by about 60 craftsmen. The longest tableaux will be 650ft and it is expected that before the display ends on October 26 the illuminations will have been seen by more than three million people.

At Morecambe the illuminations shine in Happy Mount Park and there is floodlighting for three and a half miles along the promenade. There are illuminations at Southport throughout the year, but the more spectacular pier illuminations are only for the autumn. Southend has its best illuminations since the war and of the 95,000 lamps in use more than 25,000 are on the pier. At Bournemouth, apart from the illuminations along the sea front, there are the candlelight displays where about 30,000 candles are used and are lit by tapers distributed among holiday makers. Brighton, Eastbourne, Torquay, Paignton and Margate all vie for the visitors and are decked out with twinkling lights, gardens, flower beds and fountains shimmer in multi-colours and promenades are lit with thousands of lamps.

SEPT 3RD - 9TH 1953

IN THE NEWS

Thursday 3   **"Lights On For Radio Show"** The Radio Show opened at Earl's Court in half-light yesterday, but most of the electricians who have been on strike resumed work last night. There are still 2,000 electricians on strike.

Friday 4   **"Strikes at Five Power Plants"** Many more electricians have joined in the strikes called by the Electrical Trades and among the sites affected were extensions to four power stations in London and one near Brighton. A spokesman of the British Electricity Authority said that the stoppage would have no effect on electricity supplies.

Saturday 5   **"Dr Adenauer's Pre-Election Surprise"** The West German chancellor has proposed a non-aggression pact with Russia to meet Soviet security demands half-way.

Sunday 6   **"Final Exchange in Korea"** The exchange of prisoners of war came to an end. The Communists sent back 12,751 UN prisoners, while the UN returned 74,000 Chinese and North Koreans.

Monday 7   **"Duke Does It"** In Britain, Chief test pilot, Squadron Leader Neville Duke, established a new world air speed record in a Hawker Hunter with an average speed of 727.6mph.

Tuesday 8   **"Absolute Majority for Dr Adenauer"** The Federal German Chancellor has an absolute majority of one in the new Bundestag. He said this would bring new impetus to the efforts to build the European Political and Defence Communities.

Wednesday 9   **"Breaking the Sound Barrier"** Before he came visible, loud 'supersonic bangs' announced the arrival over the Farnborough Air Show of Squadron Leader Neville Duke in the Hawker Hunter in which he set the world speed record on Monday.

HERE IN BRITAIN

"Two On a Line"

The shared telephone service has problems. There are 600,000 subscribers, most of whom have separate accounts, but many do not. Subscriber A must work out with Subscriber B the number of local calls made, because any calls above the 'normal number' are charged to one of the sharers and he must then collect moneys due to him from the other subscriber. Subscribers complain of overhearing, when the line is in use by the other subscriber, every word can be heard. One solicitor says he has to warn local clients that their matrimonial or business affairs are not a subject for discussion on a shared line.

AROUND THE WORLD

"Drifting Across the Atlantic"

The yacht 'Petula' sailed from Plymouth carrying three marine biologists whose intention is to drift 2,500 miles across the Atlantic, as slowly as possible, to observe the sea's surface. Their first port of call will be Dakar, in north-west Africa, where a balsa wood raft is waiting to be towed as a platform for fishing and photography, and from where they will set off for the West Indies. In addition to making weather reports, photographing birds and catching fish, the party will take samples of sea and air, put into a thousand glass jars for analysis when they get back next year.

BRIDGING THE GANGES

The Indian railway board announced that preliminary work on a £12m project to bridge the Ganges 50 miles east of Patna begins this month. This bridge will link India's two most important railway systems - the eastern railway and the north-eastern railway and also, open up the coal and iron resources of northern Bihar. This scheme has been under consideration since the days of British rule to end the bottleneck crossing the Ganges in eastern India caused by having to rely on a ferry across the river. The cost of the bridge is expected to be about £5m and another £2 will be needed for protection works on the banks of the 'mighty Ganges'. As the gauges of the railways on each side are different a new trans-shipment yard on one side will be required and other ancillary works will bring the total expenditure up to about £12m.

The most difficult part of the project will be a bund, over one mile long and a 70ft high, two miles long approach bank on the north side, both of which will have to be completed simultaneously from start to finish within about six months. The Indian railway board believes that *'nothing on quite this scale within the time permitted has been attempted in the way of river control in India or elsewhere so far.'* The Board anticipates the bridge will have spans of about 600ft to keep the number of piers to the minimum, having learned lessons from the 1934 Bihar earthquake special attention has to be paid to the foundations, but the firms, including British concerns, tendering for the project will have a chance to suggest their alternative designs as the bridge will be almost 6,000 ft long.

SEPT 10TH-16TH 1953

IN THE NEWS

Thursday 10   **"Communist Action off Hong Kong"** Six crew of a Royal Navy motor launch on patrol duty in the Pearl River estuary 20 miles from Hong Kong, were killed and five others wounded, when they were fired on by a Chinese Communist vessel.

Friday 11   **"Earthquake in Cyprus"** Cyprus experienced its most severe earthquake for centuries. 40 people are known to have died and some 1,500 are homeless.

Saturday 12   **"Chinese Reach 'Peace Town'"** The first 1,000 Chinese Korean prisoners of war, who do not want to return home, entered the demilitarised zone and were taken into custody by Indian troops. Many shouted "Death to the Communists".

Sunday 13   **"Russians Reject Berlin Air Pact"** Russia has refused to give an undertaking that they will not fire on Allied planes straying from the Berlin air corridor on their way to Allied bases.

Monday 14   **"NATO War Ships Exercise"** Operation 'Mariner' is being held from the Arctic to the Mediterranean. Some 300 warships of nine NATO countries, plus 1,000 aircraft and half a million officers and men will take part in the largest ever combined manoeuvres.

Tuesday 15   **"Battle of Britain Fly Past"** Thousands watched the largest number of jet aircraft ever to fly over the capital together. Led by a veteran Hurricane and Spitfire to commemorate the Battle of Britain, 252 aircraft flew in 11 formations from Southend to Whitehall.

Wednesday 16   **"Return to Work Sought"** The 4,300 electricians, on strike since August 24th, are told by their union to resume work tomorrow, when a court of inquiry appointed by the Minister of Labour begins.

HERE IN BRITAIN

"Battle for the Baby Car"

Britain's answer to the challenge of small Continental cars began on the world market this week with the launch of the 'Standard Eight'. The 8hp Standard is the lowest priced four cylinder, four-seater, four-door, four-speed saloon model on the market.

The basic price is £339, plus £142 7s. 6d. purchase tax, making a total of £481 7s. 6d. The car is already being produced in volume and supplies have been delivered to distributors and dealers throughout the world. By the end of the year the output should reach 1,000 cars a week and production was planned eventually to reach 2,000 cars a week.

AROUND THE WORLD

"Cyprus Hit By Quake"

The earthquake in Cyprus devastated villages in the Paphos district, the most seriously damaged ones were Stroumbi and Kidassi where virtually no houses were left standing. The shock was also felt in Nicosia but caused no injuries or damage, however, houses trembled, and furniture rattled, making alarmed citizens rush into the streets in pyjamas and dressing gowns.

As soon as news reached Nicosia of the disaster the Government took steps to send help in the shape of tents, blankets, olives, cheese and bread for distribution to the victims, while doctors, ambulances and extra police hastened to the scene to treat the injured.

WHITSTABLE OYSTERS

The annual oyster season opened in Whitstable with a simple ceremony. Carrying a party of Men of Kent – those from east Kent – one fishing boat trawled the Whitstable Oyster Company beds and the first 'dredge' of the year was eaten on board before the boat returned to harbour to be dressed overall, like other oyster craft, for a short religious service of blessing the waters.

The Whitstable oyster beds have existed since Roman times and the fisher folk of the city started the ceremony to honour the invisible powers that helped them to have an adequate, if not bumper, harvest and to keep the men safe at sea. After the shells have been cleaned by hand, the oysters are sorted into five grades. First grade is the 'Whitstable Royal' which is the most sought after, but some think the 'number five button' is the best value for money, at one-third the price of Royals, the smallness of shell is said to be no true guide to the quantity of fish within.

Oyster fishing is at the mercy of nature and, this year, there was a high proportion of 'clocks' or dead oysters which had to be jettisoned. This is attributed to heavy deposits of salt left by the January floods which, in effect, suffocated the oysters. Worryingly, it is thought the effects of the salt will remain for the next four or five years as it will inevitably have affected the young stock – sown in the nursery beds - which will be ready for dredging in years to come. Every year the demand for Whitstable oysters far outstrips the supply. Gone are the days when oysters were eaten by the working classes of London as whelks and mussels are now, the West End alone can support the industry on its present scale.

SEPT 17TH-23RD 1953

IN THE NEWS

Thursday 17   **"Disappearance of Mrs Maclean"** Melinda MacLean, the wife of spy Donald MacLean who disappeared in 1951, has herself gone missing from Geneva with her three children. It is thought she is going to join her husband in Moscow.

Friday 18   **"Guildford Train Crash"** An electric train overran the buffers at Guildford. The front coach ploughed through the station master's office trapping and injuring five of the staff. A party of schoolgirls in the front coach escaped over the pile of rubble.

Saturday 19   **"Francasal: Four Arrested"** Four men, two bookies and two racehorse owners, have been charged in connection with the 'Great Bath Racecourse Swindle' in July when two horses were 'swapped'.

Sunday 20   **"Saturday Shifts in the Pits"** Saturday working, from May to September, is subject to voluntary agreement at colliery level and production this summer months has been more than a million tons greater than last year.

Monday 21   **"Soviet Share"** Russian aid for the rehabilitation of North Korea, announced in Moscow yesterday, will cover industrial reconstruction, the provision of technical and financial assistance and the technical training of Koreans.

Tuesday 22   **"Ships Damaged in Gales"** Gales blew up over almost all the coastal districts of England, Wales, and Ireland. Ships were damaged, fishing interrupted and 'The Queen Elizabeth' was unable to dock at Southampton.

Wednesday 23   **"Price Handicap of White Loaf"** In the three weeks since Government control of the milling industry ended and the white loaf reappeared in bakers' shops after 13 years, the national loaf is still much preferred. Mainly because of its price, 1d or 2d less.

HERE IN BRITAIN

"Relic of Thomas Becket"

Ten thousand Roman Catholics made a pilgrimage to Canterbury in honour of St. Thomas of Canterbury and witnessed the return of a relic of Thomas Becket to the town in which he was martyred. The relic, a finger-bone, was a gift from Belgium and was presented to St Thomas's Church. It was carried in procession along the Penitential Mile to the cathedral gateway, the path taken by King Henry II when he went in penance for the murder of Becket, and at the church, was placed in St Thomas's shrine. A special casket will be made so that it may be venerated by future pilgrims.

AROUND THE WORLD

"Dior's Girls Hemmed In"

Christian Dior has been threatened with action because his seamstresses are working under unhygienic conditions with not enough air space. A spokesman said, "*Our 900 girls do work under impossible conditions, under stairs, on landings and down dark passages. BUT don't blame us! Blame the Ministry of Economic Affairs*". The Ministry occupies an important part of the premises Dior bought in 1948 and were supposed to move out – but they haven't – and successful M Dior, has not room to expand. In spite of all his letters of protest, the Ministry "*Have nowhere to put their control inspectors.*"

CLOTHES COST EXTRA

The rates paid for film extras has been increased in an agreement negotiated between the British Film Producers' Association and the Film Artistes' Association based on the standard agreement between the two bodies that has operated since October 1947. In particular, there are changes to the payments for 'wearing your own clothes'. The former rate of £1 a day or night for providing and wearing your own evening or morning dress is unchanged, but now, the same payment will be made for 'ultra-smart' day clothes, 'in current fashion and of high quality, with accessories thereto'.

Other special dress for which extra fees will be paid include: £1 for, "A frock coat (with or with-out silk hat), white flannels, tropical suits, Ascot clothes, beach costume (providing arms, legs and body are made up), artists' own uniform, waiters' suits, black coat and striped trousers, riding habit, full flying kit, skiing outfit, high quality Mediterranean clothes." 10s (50p) for, "Rugby or Soccer jerseys and shorts. 2s 6d (12p) for, 'Pyjamas, dressing-gown and slippers. For, "Miscellaneous dress, Fancy dress costumes and clown costumes", a fee will be negotiated. When an artist must provide and wear more than one suit in a day, he will receive a standard payment of 7s 6d (37p) for the second "and each subsequent suit so provided and worn." It is stipulated that clothes for which extra payments are made must be approved by the film company and be clean and well pressed, and linen well laundered and although the wearing of period costume, provided by the company, does not necessarily constitute a claim for extra pay, an artist may be paid 10s (50p) extra for wearing an elaborate costume, with special hairdressing, wigs and character make-up. When the costume requires "special carriage and deportment", an additional payment may be made.

SEPT 24TH-30TH 1953

IN THE NEWS

Thursday 24 **"New Row Over Death Penalty"** A recommendation that the jury should decide whether the death sentence or life imprisonment should be imposed on a prisoner found guilty of murder is made by the Royal Commission on Capital Punishment.

Friday 25 **"New Air Speed Record"** Over the Azizio plain in Libya, Lieutenant-Commander Lithgow succeeded in his first serious attempt in the Supermarine Swift F4 to establish a new world's air speed record.

Saturday 26 **"Your Doctor and You"** The British Medical Association reports that after two years' experience of the NHS, there has been some deterioration in the relationship between doctor and patient - because some patients make unreasonable demands.

Sunday 27 **"Sugar Rationing Ends"** All controls over the distribution, use and prices of sugar, syrup, and treacle removed and restrictions on the use of sugar for manufactured foods, such as cakes, biscuits and sweets, were taken off.

Monday 28 **"Anglia and Prefect Join In"** Fords announced their new 'Anglia' and new 'Prefect', 2-door and 4-door respectively, to meet the growing competition at home and abroad in the small car market.

Tuesday 29 **"British Rail Blushes"** Trouble flared over the mixing of men and women in some BR 'sleepers'. This time complaints came from strangers who had to share compartments in 'The Tynesider', the night express from Kings Cross to Newcastle-on-Tyne.

Wednesday 30 **"Soviet's Disagree"** Moscow has made a reply to the western proposal for a four-Power conference at Lugano in October with counter proposals for two conferences. One of four Powers on Germany and of five Powers, including China, on the Far East.

HERE IN BRITAIN

"Unlucky for Some"

One of the four men charged with stealing £3,000 cash and jewellery valued at £29,000 from Maple and Co., furnishers in Tottenham Court Road, at the beginning of the week, was stopped by police, carrying a bag containing a large quantity of money. He attributed his bad luck at being caught so quickly to his superstitions. *"I took the unlucky opal"*, he said, *"and then I booked into room 13 at my digs. I might have guessed this was coming to me."* One of his accomplices was equally unlucky, when police searched his home his wife said, *"I warned you, I shall tell them if you don't."*

AROUND THE WORLD

"Piccard Goes Further Down"

A month after his dive off Capri, Professor Piccard accompanied by his son, in his Italian-built bathyscaphe, touched the bottom of the 'Tyrrhenian pit', one of the deepest parts of the sea around the shores of Italy. He reached almost 10,000ft to make it the deepest dive on record. The diving bell was under water for exactly two hours and 15 minutes. On surfacing, he said, *"The darkness was absolute, and our powerful searchlight did little to relieve the gloom, but minute points of phosphorescent light pricked the darkness, proving that there was some kind of life down there".*

WORLD AIR SPEED WARS

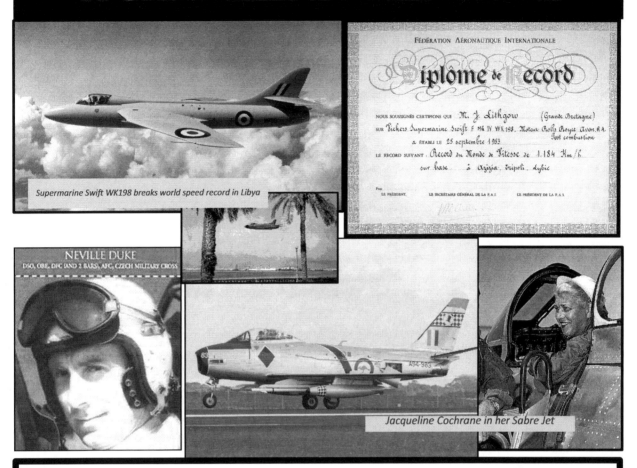

Supermarine Swift WK198 breaks world speed record in Libya

NEVILLE DUKE
DSO, OBE, DFC (AND 2 BARS), AFC, CZECH MILITARY CROSS

Jacqueline Cochrane in her Sabre Jet

The official air speed record over a 100-kilometre (62.4 miles) closed circuit course was set by Jacqueline Cochrane of the US in May with a speed of 652.55mph in a Sabre Jet at Edwards Air Base, California. Next came an unconfirmed American record on 1st September by Brigadier-General Holtoner, of the USAF, with a speed of 690.12mph also in a Sabre Jet. *"Established in a heat wave and the best possible flying conditions".*

Then it was Squadron Leader Neville Duke's turn. He broke both these records near Dunsfold in Surrey, in a Hawker Hunter flying over the 62-mile course *"in the worst possible flying conditions-low cloud, high wind and driving rain."* This was followed quickly on 7th September, when in the same aircraft, Duke set up a new world speed record of 727.6 mph at Littlehampton in Sussex.

Duke had performed a victory roll over Vickers Armstrong Ltd., who announced their attempt by the Vickers Supermarine Swift F4 on this new world air speed record, would take place near Castel Idris, Libya, the following week. So only days after Neville Duke established a new world air speed record in Britain, Lieutenant Commander Lithgow broke it over the shimmering desert in Libya.

These sub-tropical conditions showed that great heat is a mixed blessing as whilst allowing higher speeds to be established, the high temperatures were responsible for many technical difficulties, both in the aircraft and on the ground. All the dry ice taken out from England was of little avail against the burning sun and the 180 degrees in the cockpit which *'nearly roasted'* the pilot. Problems with instruments and a 'bumpy' ride over the Garian hills slowed him down on some runs, but one of the Swift's earliest attempts at a speed of 737.3 miles an hour, was claimed as the new world speed record.

IN THE NEWS

Thursday 1   **"Labour Vote Against"** The Labour Party, at its annual conference at Margate, rejected nationalisation of the land and also rejected widening the policy of nationalisation by including engineering and other industries in the party's proposals.

Friday 2   **"TV Joins in Murder Hunt"** For the first time ever, BBC television was called in to help Scotland Yard in a murder inquiry and the face of a man wanted for questioning in connection with a murder was shown on British television.

Saturday 3   **"More Rioting in Korea"** Frustrated by the delay in examining the cases of the prisoners of war who have refused repatriation, violence has broken out again. Indian guards fired on prisoners who were attempting to escape from their temporary holding camp.

Sunday 4   **"Clothing Added to East German Parcels"** Approximately 5 million parcels, valued at more than 27m marks, have been given out in west Berlin. The East Germans still come in crowds to collect them and and warm clothing will now be included.

Monday 5   **"Mr Eden Returns"** He resumes his duties as Secretary of State for Foreign Affairs after six months' absence through illness.

Tuesday 6   **"Britain Sends Troops to Guiana"** Naval and military forces have been sent to British Guiana; the constitution has been suspended to prevent Communist subversion and a state of emergency declared.

Wednesday 7   **"Petrol Down ½d Today"** Five petrol companies reduced the prices of their standard grade petrol. Premier grades remain unchanged, Shell-Mex and BP charge 4s 5½d a gallon (4p a litre)

HERE IN BRITAIN

"Hero of the Princess Victoria"

The George Cross was posthumously awarded to Radio Officer David Broadfoot, of the ferry 'Princess Victoria', which sank off the Irish coast in January with the loss of 133 lives. The citation states that he *"deliberately sacrificed his own life in an attempt to save others. RO Broadfoot constantly sent out wireless messages giving the ship's position and asking for assistance. When the order to abandon ship was given, thinking only of saving the lives of passengers and crew, he remained in the WIT cabin, receiving and sending messages, although he must have known that if he did this, he had no chance of surviving".*

AROUND THE WORLD

"Paris Motor Show"

When the doors of the Grand Palais opened the surprise exhibit, without which no Salon de l'Automobile would be complete, was a most unusual car, the Joymobile. To be made in Holland, it has an automatic transmission with no clutch and no gearbox and will have a plastic saloon body. The experimental X-100 car produced by the Lincoln division of the American Ford company is also attracting huge attention. Its' 'rain cells' which automatically close the sliding roof and the windows at the first drops of a shower, show that Henry Ford's saying, *"I refuse to recognize the existence of impossibilities"*, is alive and well.

JUNK PLAYGROUNDS

In the 1950s most urban children played in the street outside their own home. There was not much traffic but large groups of noisy children annoyed the inhabitants!
The junk playgrounds were open spaces where children could repair, build and play, without annoying anyone!

The benefit and pleasure given to town children of the 'junk' playground, received emphatic endorsement at Kensington this week. The Clydesdale Road adventure playground, Notting Hill, has been so successful that a national committee has been formed to encourage more playgrounds to be provided all over the country. Lady Allen of Hurtwood is the new President of the Committee and it was she who visited Denmark and witnessed first-hand the idea of a Mr Sorenson, who himself had noticed that children preferred to play anywhere and everywhere other than on traditional playgrounds. He imagined a 'junk' playground where children could use their imagination to create their own settings and built his first 'Adventure' playground. In post-war Britain it could be seen that children were more than happy to play on the old bomb sites in town, creating their own games amongst the chaos.

The Clydesdale Road ground provides a 'safer' space, where piles of rubble and sand provide for climbing and digging, flatter areas are great for building and there is even a space for building fires. Old wheelbarrows, spades and tyres are the main equipment and there seems to be no shortage of ideas for games amongst scrubby bushes and tree stumps. The playground is open only at set times, after school and longer in the holidays and at weekends and is always under supervision. It is sponsored by a voluntary committee and their task had not been without problems. There were numerous objections from other residents on account of the noise and dust but a mother from the Clydesdale Road neighbourhood summed up the beneficial effect, not only on her five-year-old daughter, coming home dirty and happy, but also on herself. For her it had changed the whole aspect of living there.

IN THE NEWS

Thursday 8 **"More Troops for Guiana"** The People's Progressive Party stated, *"We cannot see any reason for such intimidation when all Guianese know that conditions in our country are normal and peaceful. There is no disturbance, unrest or violence".*

Friday 9 **"Continuing Shortage of Dentists"** The Minister of Health warned of the most serious and persistent problems of the dental service and the hopeless insufficiency of dentists to cope with the needs of the population.

Saturday 10 **"RAF Canberra Wins the Air Race"** The longest air race ever held - nearly 12,300 miles from London to Christchurch, New Zealand - was won in an English Electric Canberra PR3 aircraft, taking 23 hours 52 minutes, including one hour 23 minutes on the ground.

Sunday 11 **"Fish on Wednesday"** George Dawson, the London scrap metal millionaire who is out to beat the ban on Icelandic fish, announced that the first landing of fish under his agreement with Iceland will be made at Grimsby on Wednesday.

Monday 12 **"Prime Minister's Return"** Sir Winston Churchill made a triumphant return to public life after his illness. He addressed a meeting of Conservatives after the party's annual conference at Margate.

Tuesday 13 **"No Crocodile Tears for George"** London Zoo's oldest alligator, George, has died. He was 11ft long and about 60 years old. He arrived at Regent's Park in June 1912.

Wednesday 14 **"Fish Price War at Grimsby"** As George Dawson prepared to market his fish caught by Icelandic trawlers, the Ross group, announced a decision to undercut Dawson's prices by 6d (2p) a stone on all classes of fish indefinitely.

HERE IN BRITAIN
"Outstanding Drive"

A Morris Minor saloon completed the journey from Rome to London in 25 hours, including one hour crossing the Channel. For the 1,038 miles from Rome to Le Touquet their average speed was 45 mph. The drivers said that their chief handicap was intermittent fog during the night run across France and that only one car passed them during the journey, which included crossing the 6,000ft Mont Cenis Pass. This performance would be creditable with a large, fast car, but with a small saloon powered by an 800cc engine it is outstanding and is high testimony of the speed and stamina of the modern British small car.

AROUND THE WORLD
"Any Old Iron?"

The Foire à la Ferraille (the old iron fair) is held in October in Paris. For about a mile along a shady Boulevard, there grows a gigantic accumulation of unwanted objects, the discarded and obsolete, the result of changing tastes or progress. Junk which has been lingering unsold in antique shops is brought here by the shop owners in a last-ditch attempt to catch somebody's fancy at a 'bargain' price. Ornaments, lamps, clocks, china and glass, all jostle for space next to coal stoves, spinning wheels or cartwheels, all of which provide vast entertainment and interest for the crowds who stroll by.

DAWSON'S FISH WAR

75 ÍSLAND

Ingólfur Arnarson

Cod on sale in Grimsby Fish Market

Twelve months ago, Iceland unilaterally extended their territorial fishing limits to twelve miles and the Grimsby Fish Merchant's Association decided to support their local fishermen in their fight against this action. No Icelandic fish was to be landed at Grimsby and, therefore, Grimsby merchants could not purchase Icelandic fish for distribution. Then along came Mr George Dawson, son of a 'Cockney' scrap metal dealer in Bermondsey, who had made his fortune after the war by selling off surplus equipment. Now a millionaire, he has turned his attention to the fishing industry and struck a deal with Iceland.

In a blaze of publicity, his first consignment of fish arrived in Grimsby just before midnight on board the Icelandic trawler, 'Ingolfur Arnarson'. She had on board, 33,000 stone, all but 5,000 stone of it 'high quality cod', half of which was on offer to the Grimsby fish merchants at auction before dawn, the other half having been loaded onto Dawson's lorries and taken to Billingsgate fish market in London. Only one Grimsby merchant purchased some of Mr Dawson's fish – he is now boycotted by the local fishermen - but many merchants from other towns turned up to purchase supplies.

By mid-morning what was left was taken off to a newly acquired factory at Pyewipe in Lincolnshire, where the floors were ready stacked with ice blocks brought from Lancashire, and it was then offered to retailers such as the Co-operative Wholesale Society, Lewis's of Manchester and Selfridge's. All had suggested they were happy to buy Icelandic fish when looking for the best quality fish at the most competitive prices. Another Icelandic trawler is expected at Grimsby next week, and meanwhile, an invitation has been received to land Icelandic fish at West Hartlepool and distribute it from there.

IN THE NEWS

Thursday 15 **"New Atom Weapon"** The 'Penney utility', Britain's second atomic test weapon has been successfully exploded at Woomera, Australia. Sir William Penney is in charge of the tests.

Friday 16 **"Fuel Possibilities of Natural Gas"** Drilling in various parts of the country to ascertain whether there are resources of natural gas which might augment the nation's supplies is to be undertaken for the Gas Council.

Saturday 17 **"530 Queue Up to Escape"** Men at Manchester's Bradford Colliery were cut off from their normal exit shaft by a fire. They waited in darkness for hours, sitting at the bottom, talking, drinking tea and eating cakes, waiting for news.

Sunday 18 **"Eternal Wreaths at Runnymede"** The memorial to 20,000 airmen of the Commonwealth forces in the last war who have no known grave, was unveiled by the Queen yesterday. On the crest of Cooper's Hill were nearly 20,000 near relations and friends.

Monday 19 **"Dawson's Fighting Talk"** He stated that by the end of November he would bring in 12 trawlers of Icelandic fish a week. He is also to build a fish processing factory at Grimsby.

Tuesday 20 **"London's Meat"** Meat supplies are seriously threatened whilst 600 men at Smithfield Market are on strike. "Anybody Served" notices have been taken down from butchers' windows and supplies are strictly on the ration.

Wednesday 21 **"2,500 Oil Men on Strike"** An unofficial strike of employees of oil companies began in London. If it cannot be settled at once, public transport, private motorists and airlines will all be threatened by the end of the week.

HERE IN BRITAIN

"Gloster POWs Return"

Seventy-seven officers and men of the 1st Battalion, The Gloucestershire Regiment, whose heroic stand during the Imjin River battle was one of the most glorious fighting achievements of the Korean war, came ashore from the troopship 'Empire Orwell'.

They had been prisoners of war in North Korea for over two years and their commanding officer said, *"I think the men were magnificent. Under such harsh conditions, life and health are not wholly dependent on food, shelter, and clothing; it is to their own resolution and optimism that some of the credit must be given for the fact that few British soldiers died in captivity."*

AROUND THE WORLD

"Parmentier's Potatoes"

A plaque was unveiled in Paris this week in honour of Jean Antoine Augustin Parmentier, a chemist who, by his writings and experiments, introduced the pleasures of the potato to the French in the eighteenth century. This year is the 150th anniversary of Parmentier's death.

As a prisoner in Prussia during the Seven Years War he was forced to eat potatoes or starve whilst in France they were considered only animal feed. In 1748 it was forbidden to cultivate them as it was thought they caused leprosy – a law still in force during his time until 1772.

BABY BOOMER CARS

Ford Popular

Morris Minor

Austin A30

Aston Martin DB2-4 Drophead Coupe

The Duke of Edinburgh emphasised the need for a vastly improved road system when he opened the Motor Show at Earls Court. This year, he said, it was expected that 400,000 new vehicles would be put on the congested roads. After congratulating the motor industry on earning £1m a day in foreign currency, the Duke also made some criticisms of modern car design. *"Why is it,"* he asked, *"that there always seems to be a handle or a knob just opposite the driver's right knee?"*

The great exhibition hall was packed an hour after the doors opened and the rivalry of the 'baby' cars tended to monopolise the attention of most motorists and would-be motorists – understandably, as the addition of purchase tax puts the price of even the most modest car out of the reach of many. These new small cars on the Ford, Standard and Austin stands were hidden by men and women trying all the seats and examining the engines and luggage boots.

Ford resumed their position as the supplier of the lowest priced car in Britain - if not in the world - with the introduction of the Popular two door saloon. The basic price is £275 to which must be added £115 14s 2d purchase tax. In comparison, the Austin A30 two door saloon has a basic price of £335, the four-door Standard Eight sells at £339 and the Morris Minor two door saloon at £373.

At the other end of the price scale the blue Bentley Continental was surrounded by admirers and the growing number of 100 mph British cars have been added to by the introduction of the Daimler Conquest roadster, the Alvis Grey Lady saloon and the new version of the Aston Martin DB2-4 model with the drophead coupe body.

OCT 22ND - 28TH 1953

IN THE NEWS

Thursday 22   **"Many Garages Without Supplies"** Troops are to be considered as tanker crews if the unofficial strike of petrol distribution workers in London continues. Most bus and coach services are at risk and a rush for fuel has left London without petrol.

Friday 23   **"Crew Chosen for Royal Flight"** The Queen and the Duke of Edinburgh will fly from London Airport to Bermuda and Jamaica on the start of their Commonwealth Tour next month in a BOAC Stratocruiser airliner flown by Captain Loraine, one of the corporation's most experienced pilots.

Saturday 24   **"2,000 Troops Arrive to Drive Tankers"** At Jarrow about 160 drivers and maintenance workers at the Shell-Mex and B.P. depots have joined in the strike and fuel shortages are likely to arise in the Newcastle upon Tyne and Gateshead areas.

Sunday 25   **"Pettit Found Dead"** The man hunted for six weeks by 60,000 policemen, and who was the first murder suspect ever to be shown on television, was found dead with a confession in his pocket.

Monday 26   **"90 Years Ago Today"** On October 26,1863, the Football Association was formed of eleven clubs in the Freemasons' Tavern, Great Queen Street, London. The beginning of organised football within the British Isles.

Tuesday 27   **"Oil Strikers Back Today"** A return to work was made with a promise that the army would be withdrawn from the depots. Supplies should be fully restored within a few days.

Wednesday 28   **"VC and DSO"** Lieutenant-Colonel Carne was invested yesterday by the Queen for valour in Korea. *"He showed powers of leadership which can seldom have been surpassed in the history of our Army."*

HERE IN BRITAIN

"Trinity House Bell"

When the Queen opened the new Trinity House on Tower Hill, she was presented by the Corporation with a ship's bell for the royal yacht Britannia, in which she and the Duke of Edinburgh will sail for part of their voyage to Australia and New Zealand. Her Majesty struck a single stroke on the bell, where it hung in its polished oak frame. The bell was cast in the royal dockyard at Portsmouth and bears an inscription, with the Queen's monogram and 'HM Yacht Britannia, 1953.' The lanyard which moves the clapper has been plaited by a Trinity House rigger.

AROUND THE WORLD

"Kangaroos and Dingoes"

Alarmed at the damage being done in the north and north-west of the settled areas of South Australia by the rapidly increasing number of kangaroos which break down fences and eat feed required by sheep, graziers' have set up shooting parties and are now patrolling the areas. A wire netting fence, hundreds of miles long, is to be built in the south-west of Queensland to keep dingoes out of the sheep country. The dingo, or Australian wild dog, kills thousands of sheep and young calves every year. The new fence will ultimately give protection to about 18 million sheep.

90 YEARS OF FOOTBALL

LAWS
OF THE
University Foot Ball Club.

1. This Club shall be called the UNIVERSITY FOOT BALL CLUB.
2. At the commencement of the play, the ball shall be kicked off from the middle of the ground : after every goal there shall be a kick-off in the same way.

THE FOOTBALL ASSOCIATION 90th ANNIVERSARY

ENGLAND
v
REST OF THE WORLD

WEDNESDAY, OCTOBER 21st, 1953
KICK-OFF 2.30 pm
EMPIRE STADIUM
WEMBLEY
Chairman and Managing Director   SIR ARTHUR J. ELVIN, MBE
OFFICIAL PROGRAMME   ONE SHILLING

Wednesday, 21 October 1953
Football Association 90th Anniversary Celebration Match

England 4 Rest of the World 4 [2-3]

Empire Stadium, Empire Way, Wembley Park, Wembley, Middlesex
Kick-off (GMT): **2.30pm**
Attendance: '97,000' (sold-out); Receipts: '£49,598.' (a British midweek record)

England kicked-off   Ernst Ocwirk won the toss

"NGLAND COULD NEVER BE LUCKIER" *Daily Mirror*

A football match this month was arranged to celebrate the 90th anniversary of the Football Association and although the Rest of World team – all from Europe - was somewhat of a makeshift eleven, it was a memorable occasion. With the final result, 'Four All', the visitors had almost ended England's record of never losing to a continental side on home soil and the 97,000 crowd was thrilled. Football is the most popular sport in the world. From boys kicking a ball about in the street to adults who make a living from it and it has been around for centuries. However, before the FA was set up, different clubs and different schools all played to different rules which made it difficult to play against each other. The two predominant schools were Rugby and Eton. At Rugby the rules allowed you run holding the ball but at Eton, the ball was played exclusively with the feet. The game in Rugby was called 'the running game' while the game in Eton was called 'the dribbling game'.

The Cambridge Rules of 1848 were the first known set of laws laid down officially and allowed forward passes, as well as throw-ins, goal kicks and forbade running whilst holding onto the ball. The Sheffield rules of 1858, however, did allow running holding the ball. The FA was to agree on common rules that would be accepted across the country. The meeting also resulted in a standardisation of the size and weight of the ball. The game has, however, continued to develop as there was still much flexibility concerning the rules. For one thing, the number of players on the pitch could vary and uniforms were not used to distinguish the appearance of the teams. It was also common for players to wear caps – the header was yet to be a part of the game.

OCT 29TH - NOV 4TH 1953

IN THE NEWS

Thursday 29 **"Tribute to the Queen Mother"** Queen Elizabeth the Queen Mother was welcomed to the City of London with deep affection when she went to Guildhall to receive the freedom of the City.

Friday 30 **"Tourist Travel Allowance Increased"** The foreign currency allowance for tourists is to be increased from £40 to £50. The unlimited allowance for travel in Scandinavian countries, withdrawn in 1952, will be restored.

Saturday 31 **"Anti-Submarine Helicopters"** The Fleet Air Arm's first squadron of Westland-Sikorsky S55 helicopters left Gosport for Eglinton, in Northern Ireland, where they will begin trials with special equipment. The aircraft are similar to those now in service in Malaya.

Sunday Nov 1 **"All November's Rain in a Day"** After one of the driest Octobers for years, heavy rain and gales marked the beginning of November.

Monday 2 **"Pakistan to be An Islamic Republic"** The Constituent Assembly in Karachi decided that the country should be known as the 'Islamic Republic of Pakistan.' The future relationship with other Commonwealth countries has still to be worked out.

Tuesday 3 **"State Opening of Parliament"** The Queen outlined the Government's new housing campaign in her speech. Later, the Prime Minister appealed to Parliament to treat the provision of 'decent homes for the people' as an issue on which all parties should unite.

Wednesday 4 **"Nearing 300,000 Houses"** The Government is likely to achieve their aim of building 300,000 houses this year. For the first nine months of this year 225,863 houses were built in Great Britain, compared with 171,093 in the same period last year.

HERE IN BRITAIN

"The Weather at Sea"

Six passengers were slightly hurt when the liner Queen Elizabeth ran into gales during the last part of her voyage from New York before she docked at Southampton on schedule last night. There was a heavy sea with swells of about 40ft. At night during the crossing, passengers wedged themselves into their bunks with pillows. Safety lines were rigged in the ship and dances and other social functions were cancelled. Further north, after a tow of 130 miles, which took 30 hours in a southerly gale and rough seas, the Grimsby trawler 'Churchill' brought another trawler, the 'Coventry City' safely into Scrabster, Caithness.

AROUND THE WORLD

"Miss Smythe's Victory"

Pat Smythe, of the British equestrian team visiting the US and Canada, won the first international jumping event at the Pennsylvania horse show in a field that contained some of the world's top male riders.

Miss Smythe, the first woman from abroad to compete in this country was thrown by her mount 'Tosea' in the second round, but quickly recovered and rode the final round on 'Prince Hal' without a fault. Great interest is being taken in the British team, as winners of the last Olympic championship, before they go to New York for the National Horse Show at Madison Square Garden.

FREEDOM OF THE CITY

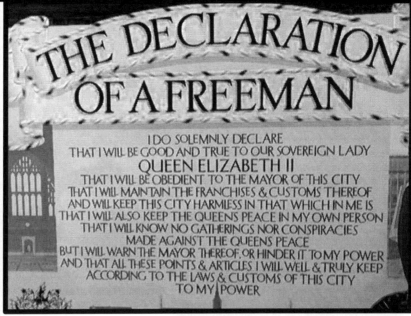

THE DECLARATION OF A FREEMAN

I DO SOLEMNLY DECLARE
THAT I WILL BE GOOD AND TRUE TO OUR SOVEREIGN LADY
QUEEN ELIZABETH II
THAT I WILL BE OBEDIENT TO THE MAYOR OF THIS CITY
THAT I WILL MAINTAIN THE FRANCHISES & CUSTOMS THEREOF
AND WILL KEEP THIS CITY HARMLESS IN THAT WHICH IN ME IS
THAT I WILL ALSO KEEP THE QUEENS PEACE IN MY OWN PERSON
THAT I WILL KNOW NO GATHERINGS NOR CONSPIRACIES
MADE AGAINST THE QUEENS PEACE
BUT I WILL WARN THE MAYOR THEREOF, OR HINDER IT TO MY POWER
AND THAT ALL THESE POINTS & ARTICLES I WILL WELL & TRULY KEEP
ACCORDING TO THE LAWS & CUSTOMS OF THIS CITY
TO MY POWER

The Freedom of the City of London confers the right to drive sheep over London Bridge.

This week, Queen Elizabeth the Queen Mother was honoured with the Freedom of the City of London. It was, in her Majesty's own words, *'with pride and gratitude and as a sister of the Shipwrights' Company"* that she accepted. Freedom of the City was first recorded in 1237 and is closely tied to the role and status of the Livery Companies. It was, in earliest times, an essential requirement for all who wished to carry on business within the Square Mile. As a result, the privileges attaching to the Freedom were eagerly sought, while the duties and obligations of freemen were faithfully observed. The Queen Mother spoke of her love for and pride in Londoners, and concluded, "*I am proud and glad to take my place in a great company of men and women who have pledged themselves to your ideals of Christian service. In accepting the freedom of the City of London I pledge myself anew as long as I shall live to the service of our people, our country, and our Commonwealth.*"

It is still necessary to this day for all liverymen to be freemen of the City and it is the liverymen who elect the Lord Mayor and the Sheriffs of the Corporation of London. It is no longer necessary to be a freeman to work in the City, but from 1835, the freedom 'without the intervention of a Livery Company' could be purchased by nomination of two sponsors for a fee, known as a 'fine', of (now) £100, and is free to those on the electoral roll of the City. There are a number of rights traditionally but apocryphally associated with freemen including the right to drive sheep and cattle over London Bridge and carry a naked sword in public. However, these privileges are now effectively symbolic.

Nov 5TH - 11TH 1953

IN THE NEWS

Thursday 5 "Grave Riots in Trieste" For the first time in their eight years' occupation, Allied troops were called out in force. Pro Italian crowds surged through the city yelling, 'English get out'. Three people were killed when police opened fire.

Friday 6 "Guy Fawkes Day Rags" Guy Fawkes night in London was the most violent since pre-war days, mainly because of unofficial protests by students against the cancellation of their traditional November 5 rag.

Saturday 7 "Use of Princess Flying Boats" With a more powerful Bristol Proteus engine becoming available, BOAC have been re-examining with Saunders-Roe, the future development of the 140-ton Princess, the largest aircraft yet made in this country.

Sunday 8 "Remembrance Day" In Whitehall, the Queen led the tributes when she laid a wreath on the Cenotaph in honour of those who gave their lives in the two great wars.

Monday 9 "Signor Pella Demands Inquiry" Italians are placing the blame for the riots in Trieste last week on the British authorities. The Italian Prime Minister demanded an inquiry into the shooting of six demonstrators.

Tuesday 10 "Atomic Energy Board" Responsibility for atomic energy development is to be transferred from the Minister of Supply to a new Corporation and Sir Edwin Plowden will be appointed its first chairman.

Wednesday 11 "Bermuda Conference" The three-Power conference at Bermuda, which was to have been held in July, will now take place in December. Sir Winston Churchill, President Eisenhower and M Laniel of France will put the future of Germany and Austria at the forefront of their discussions.

HERE IN BRITAIN
"Shilling-a-Tail"

Over 257,000 grey squirrels were killed in Britain during the past 12 months. Following the first anti-grey squirrel propaganda on Radio 4s 'The Archers', this is 90,000 more than the previous year and is due to the campaign announced in March, introducing bonus system to complement the 7,000 squirrel shooting clubs - one shilling or two free cartridges paid per grey squirrel tail. The Forestry Commission has issued about £6,500 in 'shilling-a-tail' rewards so far. Since their release in 1890 at Woburn and in the absence of competition and predators, the grey squirrel population has exploded.

AROUND THE WORLD
"Dutch Seal Last Flood Gap In Dyke"

In the Netherlands, to the accompaniment of whistles, bells and loud cheers, the fourth and final caisson was successfully sunk in the Ouwerkerk gap, the last through which the tide had still flowed following the disastrous floods in February. This last of the four Phoenix caisson had been pushed very slowly into place by nine tugboats and up to the last minute, nobody knew whether the extremely difficult operation would meet with success. The tide, which runs normally at about 6ft a second, had quickened through the narrowing of the gap to nearly 9ft a second, and at times to over 12ft.

QUEEN IN A GOTHIC REVIVAL

This passenger lounge was converted to be the Queens private lounge

The SS Gothic flying the Royal Ensign on the prow.

The liner 'Gothic', in which the Queen and the Duke of Edinburgh are sailing on their tour of the Commonwealth, left London for Jamaica where the Royal couple joined her. The accommodation has been prepared for the tour and is now as it was when 'Gothic' sailed early last year for the royal tour which was cancelled because of the death of King George VI.

The personal state rooms for her Majesty and the Duke of Edinburgh are situated aft on the level of the boat deck. Immediately below, on the promenade deck level, the smoking room has been partitioned to provide the Queen's day cabin on the starboard side and the Duke of Edinburgh's day cabin on the port side. The Queen's day cabin has off-white walls, pale turquoise curtains and silver wall lights. The settee suites are covered with unglazed chintz. The Duke of Edinburgh's day cabin contains a mahogany writing desk used by Queen Victoria in the royal yacht 'Victoria and Albert'. Both day cabins are carpeted in dove grey, and each has an oxidised silver fireplace.

In the lobby forward of the central vestibule is an illuminated wall map on which the route of the tour is traced in coloured light and on which the ship's position on any day can be shown. The veranda cafe immediately aft the day cabins will be used as a veranda by the Queen and the Duke of Edinburgh and is furnished with oak tables and chairs upholstered in blue and dark red.

On the saloon deck the dining saloon has been divided and now consists of the royal dining cabin on the starboard side and the lounge has been similarly divided.

The 45ft royal barge is stowed in the after well-deck and is that used by King George VI during his tour of South Africa in 1947.

Nov 12TH - 18TH 1953

IN THE NEWS

Thursday 12 **"Cleaner Food Bill"** Powers to register all premises where food is sold or handled are proposed in the Food and Drugs Amendment Bill. The criteria for registration will depend on the construction, equipment and cleanliness of premises.

Friday 13 **"Health Service Fog Masks"** Doctors are to prescribe masks for people who suffer from heart or lung disease and who live or work where smoke-polluted fog is likely to occur.

Saturday 14 **"Pork Flu Warning"** A rare Eastern disease has claimed hundreds of victims in Liverpool. Trichinosis is similar to flu and a consignment of pork is believed to be 'the carrier'.

Sunday 15 **"Commercial TV Planned for Next Year"** Britain's first commercial television stations are expected to open in London, Birmingham and Manchester. A public corporation will own and operate stations, controlled by directors appointed by the Government, and the companies will be responsible for the programmes.

Monday 16 **"Partition Solution to Trieste Dispute"** Marshal Tito of Yugoslavia offered to divide 'Zone A' of Trieste with Italy on racial lines. In Rome, where such a solution has already been advocated, the trend of the speech was regarded as conciliatory.

Tuesday 17 **"Twenty Die in Channel Collision"** Twenty Italian sailors, including the Master, died following a collision between their steamer 'Vittoria Claudia' and a French motor vessel, 'Perou' in the English Channel.

Wednesday 18 **"Britain Wins at International Court"** A lawsuit which has been going on, with intervals, since 1066 was settled when an international court agreed that the Channel 'Islets', the oyster rocks in the Channel, the Minquiers and Ecréhous, were British.

HERE IN BRITAIN

"The Enriching Culture of TV"

"Television has enriched family life and brought to many homes an element of culture which previously has been absent." A survey to find the impact of television on the whole family, said their findings, *'should allay the fears of those who have claimed that television induces people to become mentally and physically lazy.'* It was an educational agent, particularly for those who had not passed beyond the primary schools. Topical and current affairs, plays, opera, and ballet were frequently mentioned as subjects of new interest to viewers and there was no evidence that viewers allowed themselves to become *'slaves of the television screen'*.

AROUND THE WORLD

"US Anti-Polio Vaccine Trials"

The National Foundation for Infantile Paralysis has arranged to inoculate as many as a million children with the new vaccine for protection against poliomyelitis. The vaccine was developed by Dr Jonas Salk, of the University of Pittsburgh, from a virus grown in test tubes on monkey kidney tissues. It incorporates all three types of the virus that causes poliomyelitis in human beings and so far, he has tested his vaccine on 700 children and found that it creates antibodies against all three types of the poliomyelitis virus. Some children inoculated a year ago have been shown to be still protected against the disease.

CYCLES FOR LADIES

The twenty-eighth cycle and motorcycle show was opened at Earls Court by Mr Eden, the Foreign Secretary. He said that it was many years since he had owned or ridden a motorcycle, but his wife was still the proud owner of a bicycle. *'Occasionally I see her looking enviously at those people who go chug-chugging past her with a little auxiliary assistance,'* he said. He went on to say that British machines were supreme in the world, and although they had lately been meeting strong competition, he was confident that our manufacturers were going to ensure that next year we would maintain our leadership in racing machines. The Show boasted a fair degree of innovation and ever more stylish displays and was dominated by the British firms again.

The best markets for motorcycles are the United States, Sweden, and Australia. Motorcycle sales in the United States have risen from about 100 a year before the war to a steady sale of 6,000 machines a year. Norton sprung a sporting surprise with an appearance of its famous 'kneeler' on which Rhodesian, Ray Amm, had claimed 61 speed records in France.

The manufacture of bicycles is now running at about three million machines a year, two million of which are exported, the three leading markets being British West Africa, the United States and Malaya. Before the war Britain exported 3,000 or 4,000 bicycles a year to the United States and this year the total is expected to be about 350,000. On show was a special bicycle designed for 'Ladies Only', no crossbar and a shopping basket on the front, also, a tandem plus one, a cycle to be ridden by three people. The Hercules Company took an American order for lightweight machines valued at $6m. (about £2,14m), and another order for about £1m from Persia.

Nov 19th-25th 1953

IN THE NEWS

Thursday 19   **"Unidentified Flying Object"** The Air Ministry are investigating the sighting of a 'strange object' in the sky over south-east England. It was reported by the pilot and navigator of an RAF Vampire night fighter flying at about 20,000ft and, also, by the crew of a Heavy Anti-Aircraft Regiment radar unit.

Friday 20   **"Dec 2nd is Strike Day"** The Confederation of Shipbuilding and Engineering Unions have decided to call a 24-hour strike in protest at the rejection of their claim for a 15% increase in wages. About two million workers are affected.

Saturday 21   **"Piltdown Man Forgery"** The startling discovery that one of the most famous of anthropological specimens, the Piltdown skull, is a forgery has been made by the Department of Geology at the British Museum.

Sunday 22   **"New Outbreaks of Myxomatosis"** The viral disease, which has destroyed the rabbit population of Australia and France, has been confirmed in two more Sussex locations. The Ministry of Agriculture said every effort should be made to control out-breaks.

Monday 23   **"Queen and Duke Leave on Commonwealth Tour"** The Royals flew from Heathrow to Bermuda to begin the first journey round the world by a reigning Sovereign.

Tuesday 24   **"Cow Beef Refused"** Butchers have refused to accept imported cow beef for the meat ration. London butchers are *'tired of foisting poor quality meat on the public and feel that the time has come to make a firm stand against it.'*

Wednesday 25   **"Bid to Blast Power Lines"** Border police are investigating evidence of two attempts to interrupt electricity supplies between Scotland and England by blowing up electric pylons which carry the supply between the two countries.

HERE IN BRITAIN
"Floodlit Farewell"

Thousands of people stood and waved to the Queen and the Duke of Edinburgh as they left London Airport this week at the start of their Commonwealth tour. Queen Elizabeth the Queen Mother, Princess Margaret, other members of the Royal Family, Sir Winston Churchill and members of the Cabinet, all stood waving as the airliner took off for Bermuda and thousands more watched on television in their own homes. Floodlights and arc lights lit the Queen's red-carpeted path to the aircraft Canopus. Bermuda is the first stop and the tour will continue until May next year.

AROUND THE WORLD
"Effects of Myxomatosis"

British farmers could think myxomatosis is a good thing as rabbits do so much costly damage to arable crops and pasture.
A study during 1952-53, showed myxomatosis resulted in increased production to the value of more than £30m in the sheep industry alone. Australian wool production reached an all-time record from increased sheep numbers, extension of improved pastures, and a reduction in the competition for pasture. Where the incidence of myxomatosis has been greatest the wool clip has increased most, particularly in New South Wales, Victoria, and South Australia.

SAVE WESTMINSTER ABBEY

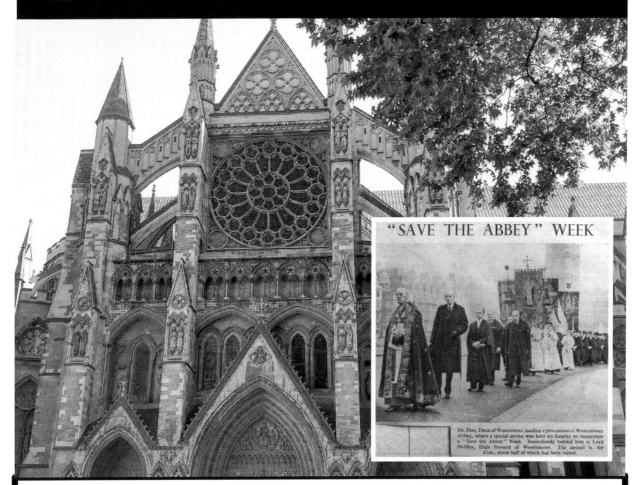

"SAVE THE ABBEY" WEEK

Dr. Don, Dean of Westminster, leading a procession to Westminster Abbey, where a special service was held on Sunday to inaugurate a "Save the Abbey" Week. Immediately behind him is Lord Halifax, High Steward of Westminster. The appeal is for £1m, about half of which has been raised.

Back in January, the Prime Minister, Winston Churchill issued a public appeal for donations to restore Westminster Abbey. He asked for 1million people to give £1 each, to save the abbey from decay and ruin. The Queen was the first to donate £1. This week at a special service in the Abbey, the Arch Deacon of Westminster commended a new appeal, 'Save the Abbey' Week, written by Sir Winston because so far, not even half the goal of £1m has been reached. The appeal was always to be confined to the Coronation Year and Sir Winston wrote, *'If we cannot find our way into the hearts and into the pockets of the British public in Coronation year we never shall. We must not fail in our duty to a great national inheritance.'*

He continued, *'In medieval times Westminster Abbey was in the country, far removed from the smoke and grime of the city of London. It stood midway between the villages of Charing and Chelsea, towering above the Tothill Fields where grass grew fresh and green, and cattle browsed among the water meadows. In recent centuries all that has been changed, and to-day the abbey is surrounded for miles in every direction by houses and factories belching forth noxious fumes which slowly and surely penetrate beneath the surface of the stonework, disintegrating it.'*

At the evening service the Arch Deacon said that a moving feature of the appeal was the way in which the 'little people' had given. 'I have especially noticed many contributions from widows sending their 'mites' and old age pensioners' gifts which must have involved severe self-denial."
After three days, a 'tremendous sum' of money had been received in thousands of letters containing gifts and many large overseas donations too, putting the fund well on the way to its target.

IN THE NEWS

Thursday 26   **"New Plans for Mines"** The minimum age of employment for boys below ground is to be raised to 16 and all youths under 18, including surface workers, will have maximum daily and weekly hours (nine hours a day and 48 hours a week) and prohibition on night work.

Friday 27   **"Lords Vote for Commercial Television"**
Peers have backed the Conservative Government's proposals for the introduction of commercial television - despite fierce opposition from some rebels.

Saturday 28   **"The Commonwealth Tour"** The Queen and the Duke of Edinburgh are now aboard 'The Gothic' and have left Jamaica, via the Panama Canal and are en route Fiji.

Sunday 29   **"Russian Shift in Strategy"** The Soviet Government has sent a Note, accepting the proposal for a four-Power conference which the western Powers have been making throughout the summer and autumn, but states that the Russians will put forward the question of calling a five-Power conference to include China.

Monday 30   **"Scotland Yard Takeover"** Yard officials may take over responsibility for all mail carried by road and rail following the breakdown of Post Office security measures after a dozen raids in the past two years.

Tuesday Dec 1 **"Britain Deposes Ruler"** The Government has withdrawn recognition from the African ruler of Buganda, a British Colony in the Uganda Protectorate, and have required him to leave the country. A state of emergency has been declared.

Wednesday 2   **"Nearly 2m Answered Strike Call"** All shipyards and more than 4,000 factories were idle as men responded to their Union's call for a 24-hour strike for a 15% wage increase.

HERE IN BRITAIN

"Tube Hot Spots"

The London Tubes are getting warmer since they were first built. Today, the temperature is in the region of 73deg, compared with 51deg in the early 1900s.

Engineers have found that train brakes are the chief source of heat, which is then stored in the clay of the tunnel walls and has been gradually accumulating. 64 wheels on an eight-car train emit a lot of heat when they are braked and when braking is repeated every few minutes. The heat does not escape, it was believed when the Tubes were first built that trains would push a column of air along in front to disperse it.

AROUND THE WORLD

"Trial by Wrestling Match"

Dr. Moussadek, on trial in Iran for his part in attempting to overthrow the Shah, told the court that when he was persuaded by his friends to leave his residence when the troops outside began to bombard it, he climbed a ladder and several walls before reaching a place of comparative safety. *"I am a man of weak constitution,"* he said, *"but believe you me, when I get mad, I am as tough as they make them. Right now, I challenge the prosecutor to wrestle with me and I can assure you I will knock him down in no time, and if he beats me, he can cut off my head."* These remarks made even the Judges laugh.

SMOG FACE MASKS

Mindful of the 'Great London Smog' of December 1952, when it is estimated between 4,000 and 5,000 people died, last month, NHS doctors were allowed to prescribe masks for people who suffer from heart or lung disease and who live or work in an area where 'smoke-polluted fog' – smog - is likely to occur. Smog is a concentration of smoke particles from industrial and domestic coal fires plus sulphur dioxide - which is produced by all petrol and even by some smokeless fuel - combined with fog. Last December, the air pressure was high, the temperatures low and when fog formed, it settled at a low level, where, with no wind to blow it away, smoke and fumes become trapped.

Visitors to an exhibition in London by the Royal Sanitary Institute, were fascinated by the model of an industrial town which demonstrated this. At the flick of a switch, fog conditions are simulated; as the ground cools more quickly than the air above, as happens on cloudless winter nights, so the smoke pouring from two factory chimneys is unable to rise and forms a stagnant zone. But when the air on the ground is warmer than the upper air, as when the ground is warmed by the sun, the smoke drifts upwards and disperses. Britain is a densely populated country which discharges into the atmosphere each year over two million tons of smoke, over half a million tons of grit and over five million tons of sulphur dioxide, and half the total smoke pollution in this country comes from domestic dwellings. A deadly combination for those with respiratory problems.

The answer is known to be the removal of these pollutants and clean air rather than face masks and the Government is aware of the urgency to make London and other industrial areas, 'smoke-free zones'.

IN THE NEWS

Thursday 3   **"Gas from the Earth"** Drilling started in Yorkshire in a search for underground reserves of natural gas-a project upon which the Gas Council will spend £1m in the next five years.

Friday 4   **"Now Engineers Ban Overtime"** After last week's 24 hour strike, the Ship Building and Engineering Unions have rejected the call for a national strike, but proposed a ban on overtime and on piece work.

Saturday 5   **"4s a Week Offered to Railmen"** An immediate increase of 4s (20p) a week – roughly one fifth of what they asked for – has been awarded by the management. About 443,600 workers are affected and the award has yet to be considered by the unions.

Sunday 6   **"15 Million Volt X-Rays"** A 15 million-volt linear accelerator, stated to be the most powerful apparatus of its kind in existence for medical purposes, is to be installed at St Bartholomew's Hospital for X-ray therapy for cancer.

Monday 7   **"Crop of Trouble for Flower Growers"** Seasonal protection is to be given to flower producers. Mild days that have brought dahlias in bloom in Scotland and ripened strawberries on the south coast, are likely to cause significant winter losses.

Tuesday 8   **"Big Three Finish in Bermuda"** The five-day conference attended by President Eisenhower, Prime Minister Churchill and Premier Laniel of France, came to an end. Agreement was made for a four-power meeting to include Russia.

Wednesday 9   **"The Pope Drives Through Rome"** Tens of thousands gathered to greet the Pope when he drove to the basilica of Santa Maria Maggiore to inaugurate the first Marian year, to commemorate the centenary of the dogma of the Immaculate Conception.

HERE IN BRITAIN

"Crazy Weather for this Time of Year"

The temperature in London and some other places in the south was exceptionally mild this week. The temperature of 63deg (17C) at Kensington Palace was the highest for any part of England and Wales in December since,1920. It reached 17deg (9C) above the December average and equalled that for the end of September. This followed on from a mild, cloudy but dry November in England, with little sunshine, whilst west Wales, north-west England and most of Scotland had excess rainfall. Similar high temperatures occurred over southern France to Switzerland, Austria, western Germany, Holland and Belgium.

AROUND THE WORLD

"The Dancing Major"

In Cairo, Major Saleh Salem, the 'voice of Egypt' and the so called 'dancing major', called on British Army Medics to spend a weekend and try to cure his two-year old son of infantile paralysis. He said he did not think the Egyptian doctors could treat the boy properly. Dapper but turbulent, the Major earned his nickname when he joined Sudanese tribesmen in a ceremonial dance in his underpants. He called himself Britain's 'Public Enemy No 1' during the Suez crisis saying his people would blow up the canal if Egypt were invaded and that Suez should *'flow with rivers of blood.'*

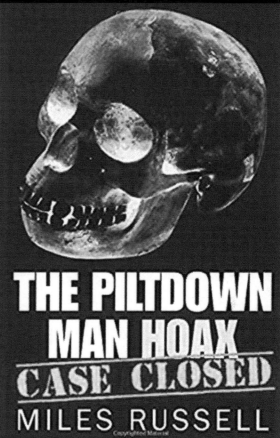

It has been discovered definitively by the Department of Geology at the British Museum, that the 'Piltdown Man' skull is a forgery. The skull was discovered, sometime around 1910-12, by Charles Dawson, a solicitor who lived in Hastings and who was an amateur collector of fossils, and who died, highly regarded by scientists, in 1916. Workmen, whom Dawson had asked to keep a look out for fossils while working in a gravel pit at Piltdown, in Sussex, found what they called a 'coconut', broke it with their pick and subsequently gave him a piece, the rest having been thrown away. Dawson recognised it as part of a very thick human skull, and he eventually found four more pieces.

Briefly, the conclusion of the scientists, from drilling the bone, using modern fluorine analysis and testing organic content, is that the fragments of the cranium are genuine remains of primitive man from the Upper Pleistocene age, about 50,000 years old. However, the large piece of mandible and the separate canine tooth are those of a modern ape, a chimpanzee or orangutan, deliberately faked to simulate fossil specimens.

Several distinguished anthropologists had previously asserted that the jaw and tooth were indeed those of an ape, albeit genuine fossils which just did not 'belong' with the skull. A modern ape was not an animal native to contemporary England and must therefore have been brought to Piltdown from elsewhere more recently. Furthermore, the jawbone had been stained with bichromate of potash and iron *'explicable only as a necessary part of the deliberate matching of the jaw with the mineralised cranial fragments,'* and in addition, the molar teeth of the mandible and the isolated canine tooth, have been artificially pared down. Never until now had it been suspected that this was a deliberate, elaborate hoax – but by whom?

IN THE NEWS

Thursday 10 **"Winston Churchill Wins Nobel Prize"** King Gustav of Sweden presented the award for Literature to Lady Churchill on behalf of her husband who was unable to attend the ceremony, being still in Bermuda.

Friday 11 **"4s Award Rejected by Rail Unions"** The three railway unions have rejected the award of an increase of 4s (20p) a week and have called for a national strike.

Saturday 12 **"Goods Piling Up"** With all the goods depots on Merseyside working to rule in protest against the recent 4s (20p) wage award, British Railways announced that they had placed an embargo on miscellaneous 'smalls traffic', except perishables and foodstuffs.

Sunday 13 **"More Myxomatosis"** Measures taken over the past two months to curtail the initial outbreaks are no longer seen to be effective. There have been several further outbreaks in south-east England.

Monday 14 **"No Russian at the Airport"** Two members of a trade delegation from Moscow arrived at London Airport unexpectedly a day early and officials could not find anyone who spoke Russian until a Soviet Embassy official arrived to meet another plane!

Tuesday 15 **"£5 Fee if BBC Runs All TV"** A two-programme service provided by the BBC, would increase the licence fee to £5 a year. The Government's proposal of a 'rival' Corporation, not drawing revenue from advertisements, would raise it to £6 or £7.

Wednesday 16 **"Rail Strike Called Off"** The threatened Christmas stoppage was abandoned after agreement was reached for the initial 4s (20p) a week rise and promises for a further improvement of standard rates of pay on a percentage basis.

HERE IN BRITAIN

"Champion Turkey for Sir Winston"

Some of the best table poultry produced for the Christmas market in Britain were displayed at the National Poultry Show at Olympia. There were over 3,000 entries including all varieties of chickens, turkeys, ducks and geese. For Christmas, good hen turkeys should cost about 6s a lb (60p/kg), and cocks, 5s (50p/kg).

A feature of the show was a display of smoked turkey, which is being offered as the cheaper but equally palatable alternative to smoked salmon. An offer for the champion table bird, a turkey weighing about 30lb, was accepted on behalf of Sir Winston Churchill to whom it will be presented.

AROUND THE WORLD

"By Car to Katmandu"

The first motor road from India to Katmandu has been opened. It is 79 miles long and winds over three successive folds of high hills. Long stretches were blasted using about 200,000lb of high explosive. Heavy bulldozers were winched across the hills and more than 800 culverts were constructed. Previously, every article imported into Nepal had been carried over the hills by coolies or hauled across on a rope-way. Motorcars, stripped of wheels and axles, were carried by large teams of coolies, who were also willing to carry travellers. Eventually, the road should increase trade between the two countries.

MACHINE THAT FLIES

WHAT THE WRIGHT BROTHERS' INVENTION HAS ACCOMPLISHED.

Americans seem to Have Solved Problem of Aerial Flight—Air Navigated Without Aid of Balloon. Built on Aeroplane Plan.

From The Car.
THE WRIGHT MACHINE.

THE INVENTORS OF THE AEROPLANE.

The first flight of the Wright Flyer, December 17, 1903, Orville piloting, Wilbur at the wingtip.

This week, Kittyhawk, N. Carolina, held the opening ceremonies of the fiftieth anniversary of the Wright brothers' first flight. The first day was pioneers' and private flyers' day, and a crowd of some 300 people assembled on top of Kill Devil Hill, where the Wright memorial stands. This austere column of granite has a circular staircase inside, and from the summit there is an uninterrupted view to the north and the scene of the Wrights' triumph. In 1903 it was a stretch of windswept sand and dunes, but now it is covered with thick grass, reeds, and bushes.

The ceremony opened with a Marine Band playing the national anthem and then a speech by Brigadier-General Frank Lahm, president of the Kill Devil Hill Memorial Society, who knew the Wrights well, making his first flight with Orville in 1908. Wreaths were laid at the foot of the memorial, 'Taps' sounded, and the procession made its way down the hill to the site of the Wrights' workshop and living quarters, now reconstructed. Close to them are the stone and marking posts of the first attempts at powered flight.

The first attempt to fly the aircraft made 50 years ago this week, because of a mishandling mishap at the start, failed. Four poles show the successful initial flights made on December 17. The first, under the control of Orville Wright, covered 100ft in 12 seconds, the second, under Wilbur Wright, made 175ft. Orville covered 200ft on the third attempt and the final flight of the day was 852ft with a duration of 59 seconds. Centre of attraction at the site is a 1912 pusher-type biplane powered by an 80 horse-power Gnome engine which will be flown over the Wright brothers' original course followed by a modern jet fighter which will attempt to break the sound barrier.

DEC 17TH - DEC 23RD 1953

IN THE NEWS

Thursday 17   **"War Canoe Escort"** The Queen and the Duke of Edinburgh arrived at the Fiji Islands aboard the Royal liner 'Gothic', exactly on time after their long voyage across the Pacific.

Friday 18   **"Huge Loss Likely on Orange Juice"** The Ministry of Food expect to lose £650,000 on the disposal of Italian concentrated orange juice found unsuitable for the welfare scheme. A local public analyst discovered that it contained more preservative than was permissible.

Saturday 19   **"Fog Over 38 Counties"** Fog persisted all day yesterday, holding up air traffic, trains and road traffic. 38 counties in England and Scotland were affected and also parts of Wales.

Sunday 20   **"Snow Comes to the Alps"** The drought that threatened to ruin the Christmas season in the Swiss winter resorts came to an end. Snowfalls of 5in to 10in are reported from many districts, but rarely below 5,000ft.

Monday 21   **"Gothic Sails for New Zealand"** The royal liner has set course for New Zealand after a brief interlude in Tonga - the 'Friendly Islands'. The Queen's visit was, in the words of the Crown Prince, *'a dream come true'*.

Tuesday 22   **"Ten Ballots in Vain"** In face of French public opinion which is turning from derision to disgust, the Congress of Parliament, made its ninth and tenth unsuccessful attempts to elect a new President of the Republic.

Wednesday 23 **"New Spurt in Industry"** More than five million tons of coal were mined last week, the best week's deep-mined output since nationalisation. Output usually rises as Christmas approaches and the miners make a special effort to increase their earnings.

HERE IN BRITAIN

"Bridge Over the Moon"

A Director of the British Astronomical Association has seen, on the moon, a bridge across a mountain barrier which looks like *'an engineering job.'* With a span of 20 miles, it is 5,000ft above plain level, a gigantic arch with a width of about a mile and a half to two miles and is perfectly regular. *'This extraordinary feature is, of course, not artificial,'* he said.

A possible explanation is that a meteorite might have crashed through a molten lava barrier and as the barrier solidified an arch was left. He found it almost incredible that such a thing could have formed in the first instance.

AROUND THE WORLD

"Prisoner Mocks the Court"

Dr Moussadek, the former Prime Minister of Iran, was sentenced to three years' solitary confinement for treason. He had been accused of defying the Shah's order to resign and of trying to overthrow the regime.

Though the prosecutor had called for the death sentence, the Shah intervened and asked that a 'not too severe' sentence should be imposed. He said, *'I forgive Moussadek because of his services during the first year of his premiership'.* But Dr Moussadek shouted out, *'I never requested clemency and will never seek it. I have done nothing wrong. You must give a verdict according to justice.'*

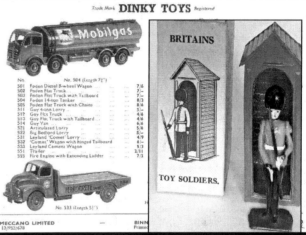

Britain is entitled to regard herself as the world's foremost toy factory. We export more toys than any other country and at home, out of every shilling now being spent in British toy shops only one penny is going into foreign manufacturers' pockets.

Judging from the splendid array of British toys now to be seen in provincial shops and in the big London stores, the toy trade was never in finer fettle. Manufacturers have been able to obtain the raw materials they want, and the result is a profusion of new and original toys, and improved versions of the old favourites, which ought to satisfy the most fastidious boy or girl. Since the war there have been complaints that the prices of toys had become too high. This Christmas the public will reap the benefit of the reduction in purchase tax from 33% to 25%. This means that a toy which last Christmas cost 10s 6d (53p) now costs 10s (50p) and there is a general tendency for prices to fall, thanks to the availability of materials.

Compared with last Christmas, toys are either cheaper or better, or both. The best of them provide some answer to occasional criticisms of shoddy construction, and toys which have come here from abroad appear inferior by comparison. The emphasis placed this year on inter-planetary travel is too plain to be missed. It seems that almost any toy can be adapted to the space-travel theme, and even the malleable face of a puppet is recognisable as that of Mr Dan Dare, that most renowned of space travellers. Sets of "space men" in 7s 6d (38p) boxes are selling well, but this does not mean that any serious threat has arisen to the existence of toy soldiers who, of course, never die.

IN THE NEWS

Thursday 24 "Lucky 13 For France" After twelve deadlocks, France has a President at last – at the 13th ballot in Versailles, Senator Rene Coty is President,

Friday 25 "The Queen's Christmas" In Auckland it was looking much like England. Christmas decorations were woven into the flags and banners; the 'Bobbie's' helmets are the same and telephone boxes painted red. Only the weather was different.

Saturday 26 "Rail Disaster in NZ" The great loss of life on Christmas Eve in the railway disaster at Tangiwai - a Maori name meaning 'Wailing Waters' - has cast its pall over the royal visit.

Sunday 27 "Date for the Four Power Conference" The Russian reply to the west suggested January 25 for the meeting in Berlin. The western Powers had proposed January 4.

Monday 28 "Round the World" Next year, tourist services will cover virtually all international routes making it possible to fly around the world for $1,100 (slightly less than £400).

Tuesday 29 "Gold by the Ton" 20 tons of gold from Moscow has been brought into London over the past four weeks, stored at the Moscow-Narodny bank.

Wednesday 30 "Flashing Light Indicators" The Ministry of Transport announced that flashing light direction indicators, seen on visiting American and Continental cars, will be legalised.

Thursday 31 "Owl Caused Power Cut" An owl sat on an oil switch at an electricity sub-station, and the lights in Gloucestershire and Monmouthshire went out for 40 minutes. The bird's wing earthed one of the phases, sending 33,000 volts through itself and creating a major fault.

HERE IN BRITAIN

"Fresh From the Mint"

New money and Christmas are traditionally associated. The Bank of England always issues millions of extra notes to meet the demand and frequently the Royal Mint has to supply extra coin. This Christmas, so far as new coin is concerned, is one of the happiest on record. Never has there been such a variety. Last year was a meagre year.

The only new coins were halfpennies and farthings and yellow threepenny bits. But 1953 is very different. Every coin has been struck for circulation with the exception of the penny. The penny has been struck only for inclusion in the special sets of coins.

AROUND THE WORLD

"New Zealand's Rail Disaster"

The cause of the accident at Tangiwai on Christmas Eve, in which 166 are feared dead, was the eruption of Mount Ruapehu, a 9,000ft volcano, which then drove a tunnel through its wall of ice and released millions of tons of water from a large lake contained within the crater.

This torrent, carrying boulders, blocks of ice and vast quantities of lava and silt, poured down the mountainside and surged into the River Whangaehu in the valley below and on to the railway bridge a few miles distant, only a few moments before the Wellington express was due to cross it.

JANUARY SALES START EARLY

SALE

Following record trade before Christmas, some stores have brought their 'sales' forward, to cash in on the benefit of any Christmas bonuses as yet unspent. Queues quickly grew outside some London shops to mark the beginning of the annual 'January' sales, whilst this year, managers boast with greater pride than usual of *'wonderful bargains'* and *'substantial reductions.'* Because of the recent mild weather, there is still a lot of winter wear remaining to be sold. Overcoats, pullovers and scarves will be sold very cheaply and bargains in footwear, notably slippers and women's boots, should also be easily found. However, it is possible the stocks of men's wear, for example, could fluctuate appreciably in the next two or three days if the post-Christmas cold weather continues.

Reductions in the price of quality raincoats are announced by one men's store in Regent Street, to be *'really colossal.'* Cotton gaberdine raincoats are reduced from 6 guineas to £3 15s and pure wool gaberdine raincoats from 13 guineas £13.65) to £8 10s (£8.50). Suit are down generally by one third. Another store had a steady stream of women walking round most floors choosing their bargains with some care. In the fashions departments there were model day and evening dresses reduced to 10 guineas, some suits and coats showed a reduction of £2 or more, and there were summer dresses at £2 10s, £3 10s and £5, and skirts at £1. Four yards of printed Tana lawn could be had for 19s 6d (97p)and 23s 6d (£1.12) and silk Noil Winton fabric for 39s 8d. Plain coloured double-width pure wool in three-yard lengths was at 69s (£3.45), 75s (£3.75) and 77s 3d (£3.95). Printed wool in four-yard lengths was at 60s (£3) and in five-yard lengths at 75s (3.75). Furnishing fabrics included cretonne, linen and damask were only slightly reduced in price.

1953 Calendar

January
S	M	T	W	T	F	S
				1	2	3
4	5	6	7	8	9	10
11	12	13	14	15	16	17
18	19	20	21	22	23	24
25	26	27	28	29	30	31

February
S	M	T	W	T	F	S
1	2	3	4	5	6	7
8	9	10	11	12	13	14
15	16	17	18	19	20	21
22	23	24	25	26	27	28

March
S	M	T	W	T	F	S
1	2	3	4	5	6	7
8	9	10	11	12	13	14
15	16	17	18	19	20	21
22	23	24	25	26	27	28
29	30	31				

April
S	M	T	W	T	F	S
			1	2	3	4
5	6	7	8	9	10	11
12	13	14	15	16	17	18
19	20	21	22	23	24	25
26	27	28	29	30		

May
S	M	T	W	T	F	S
					1	2
3	4	5	6	7	8	9
10	11	12	13	14	15	16
17	18	19	20	21	22	23
24	25	26	27	28	29	30
31						

June
S	M	T	W	T	F	S
	1	2	3	4	5	6
7	8	9	10	11	12	13
14	15	16	17	18	19	20
21	22	23	24	25	26	27
28	29	30				

July
S	M	T	W	T	F	S
			1	2	3	4
5	6	7	8	9	10	11
12	13	14	15	16	17	18
19	20	21	22	23	24	25
26	27	28	29	30	31	

August
S	M	T	W	T	F	S
						1
2	3	4	5	6	7	8
9	10	11	12	13	14	15
16	17	18	19	20	21	22
23	24	25	26	27	28	29
30	31					

September
S	M	T	W	T	F	S
		1	2	3	4	5
6	7	8	9	10	11	12
13	14	15	16	17	18	19
20	21	22	23	24	25	26
27	28	29	30			

October
S	M	T	W	T	F	S
				1	2	3
4	5	6	7	8	9	10
11	12	13	14	15	16	17
18	19	20	21	22	23	24
25	26	27	28	29	30	31

November
S	M	T	W	T	F	S
1	2	3	4	5	6	7
8	9	10	11	12	13	14
15	16	17	18	19	20	21
22	23	24	25	26	27	28
29	30					

December
S	M	T	W	T	F	S
		1	2	3	4	5
6	7	8	9	10	11	12
13	14	15	16	17	18	19
20	21	22	23	24	25	26
27	28	29	30	31		

IF YOU ENJOYED THIS BOOK PLEASE LEAVE A RATING OR REVIEW AT AMAZON